ABOUT THE EXCELLENCE OF THE GEORGIAN ENGLISH COLONY IN COMPARISON WITH OTHER COLONIES

By
Johannes Agustus Urlsperger
1747

TRANSLATED FROM THE LATIN BY
Theodora H. Miller

University Press of America,® Inc.
Lanham · Boulder · New York · Toronto · Plymouth, UK

Copyright © 2008 by
University Press of America,® Inc.
4501 Forbes Boulevard
Suite 200
Lanham, Maryland 20706
UPA Acquisitions Department (301) 459-3366

Estover Road
Plymouth PL6 7PY
United Kingdom

All rights reserved
Printed in the United States of America
British Library Cataloging in Publication Information Available

Library of Congress Control Number: 2008926471
ISBN-13: 978-0-7618-4110-4 (paperback : alk. paper)
ISBN-10: 0-7618-4110-5 (paperback : alk. paper)

∞™ The paper used in this publication meets the minimum
requirements of American National Standard for Information
Sciences—Permanence of Paper for Printed Library Materials,
ANSI Z39.48—1984

Contents

Foreword	vii
Cover Page of Translation	xi
Introduction	xiii

Purpose of Colonies
Chapter 1	1
Chapter 2	3
Chapter 3	5
Chapter 4	7
Chapter 5	9
Chapter 6	13
Chapter 7	15

Salzburgers' Journey to Georgia
Chapter 8	17
Chapter 9	19
Chapter 10	21
Chapter 11	23
Chapter 12	25

Fruitfulness of the Land
Chapter 13	27
Chapter 14	29
Chapter 15	33
Chapter 16	39
Chapter 17	43

Chapter 18	45
Chapter 19	47
Chapter 20	49
Chapter 21	53
Chapter 22	55

Trade and Economic Analysis

Chapter 23	59
Chapter 24	61
Chapter 25	63
Chapter 26	65
Chapter 27	69
Chapter 28	71
Chapter 29	73
Chapter 30	75
Chapter 31	77
Chapter 32	79

Defense and Government

Chapter 33	83
Chapter 34	85
Chapter 35	87
Chapter 36	89
Chapter 37	91
Chapter 38	93
Chapter 39	95
Chapter 40	97
Chapter 41	99
Chapter 42	101

Daily Life in Ebenezer

Chapter 43	105
Chapter 44	107
Chapter 45	109
Chapter 46	113
Chapter 47	115

Chapter 48	117
Chapter 49	119
Chapter 50	121
Epilogue	123
About the Translator	127

Foreword

This book was discovered in the basement of Halle University in Germany not so very long ago. A rare book seller sold this book to Emory University library in Atlanta, Georgia because he knew it was about Georgia. The librarian at Emory did not have anyone who was willing to translate the book. He was a friend of the Reverend Raymond Davis, a Lutheran from Savannah, who was descended from the Salzburgers. He asked Raymond if he might know someone who could do the translation. Knowing that I taught Latin, Raymond, whom I had known for a long time, asked me if I would be willing to translate it.

I have had a longstanding interest in the history of the Salzburgers. I lived in Brunswick more than thirty years (since 1968) and frequently went to St Simons Island where John and Charles Wesley preached. I also knew of the history of the Salzburgers near Savannah, so was pleased to take on this project. I had taught Latin in junior and senior high school for over 30 years in Cullman, AL and on St Simons Island, GA.

I had done a major translation previously as part of my Masters degree in Latin which I received in 1984 from the University of Georgia. I translated all the works of Hrotsvit of Gandersheim, a Saxon canoness of the tenth century who wrote six plays and several legends of the church, as well as a history of her abbey and of her father, Otto the Great. My thesis compared her work with Terence, a famous Latin playwright.[1]

In 1989 I retired from Frederica Academy on St Simons Island and began this project shortly thereafter. I took several years to do the translation because I did not work on it every day. Publication was delayed because Raymond fell ill, and I broke my hip. I would like to thank Dr. Richard LaFleur, now retired from the Classics Department at the University of Georgia, for assistance with some of the more archaic words in the manuscript. I would also like to thank John Oakley, of Ithaca, NY for help translating the German footnotes and my friends Jork and Sabine Sellschopp of Berlin, Germany for translating some of the German and Latin words that still eluded us. I thank my children, Ray and Mildred Warner, for assistance in seeing the translation through to publication.

Johannes Agustus Urlsperger wrote this book in 1747. It was written to encourage other people to come to the Georgia colony and Ebenezer in particular. Urlsperger himself did not come to Georgia, but his cousin did and went back and told Urlsperger about it. Urlsperger wrote this book as a thesis for his degree. In that day, educated people wrote in Latin.

He said Georgia had everything. In the mountains it had minerals and marble. In the plains it had plenty of room for wheat and grains. And along the coast it had plenty of room for vines for making wine and fruit. In those days there were oranges and grapefruit trees along the coast. England was particularly interested in these fruits because they could not get them from Florida since it still belonged to Spain. He also described the rich animal life (for furs) and sea life.

Urlsperger's account compared the Salzburger colony in Georgia to a colony described in Genesis. Many things are compared to scripture: the productivity of the land, and the happiness of the people. Ebenezer is compared to Pelag, who went out from the rest of his brothers and formed a colony. According to Urlsperger, to form a colony was a biblical thing to do.

This book is important because the Salzburgers, who were Lutheran, came from Salzburg, Germany when they were evicted by the King who was Roman Catholic. They traveled through Europe and people were friendly, but no one wanted them to settle in their territory. They ended up in Holland where General James Oglethorpe heard about them. He was looking for farmers to raise food for his Savannah colony, and some of the Salzburgers were farmers. Oglethorpe proposed to pay their way to the Georgia colony if they would consent to raise food for Savannah.

The Salzburgers agreed and went up the Savannah River twenty miles to make their colony which they called Ebenezer. The Salzburgers made friends with the Indians in the area, who showed them how to fish and fertilize their fields. They built a church and they had the first orphanage in the United States. Europeans had street urchins nobody wanted and the Salzburgers took them in to help in the fields. Later, they took in old people who were unwanted in Europe to look after the children, cook and make clothes for them. This was the first old folks home in the United States. Replicas of this building can be found at Ebenezer today which now serves as a Lutheran retreat. More detail on the Salzburgers can be found in the Salzburger Society of Savannah.

Theodora Heinsohn Miller
Burlington, NC
2006

Note

1. Warner, Theodora Heinsohn. 1984. Hrotsvit and Terence: A Comparative Study. Unpublished Masters Thesis, University of Georgia: Athens, GA.

Cover Page of Translation

I.N.D.

About

The excellence of the Georgian English

Colony in comparison with other colonies

With God benevolently bearing the burden of the evidence

and with the

very distinguished A.C. gathering of scholars

graciously approving

The 18th day before September A.R.S. 1747

In the morning hours

In the gloomy public field of the library

With M. Gottfried Hecking the leader (public librarian) of the Annaeani school presiding and of the Latin Society which flourishes in the German City of Jena and with the honorable colleague his own teacher and patron who is equal in all godliness and honor in a public meeting of educated men Johannes Agustus Urlspergeries will argue.

After he says greetings in a true school gymnasium of his native land and in a familiar song. (A. and R.) Augustanus Vindel of Augusta, with letters of Brinhaveriana.

Introduction

This little work is shown to you, kind Reader, because you would prefer to read it thoroughly with a just mind than to scan it lightly with sharp and harsh judgment. For I easily concede that the work is imperfect, nor is it so polished as the subject matter itself demands. Especially I very much blame the narrow limits of these pages, because either I would be forced clearly to omit very much or in no way could I follow closely from the information thus as the thing itself demands.

I shall point out very concisely here, having struggled with these testimonies; I would not hesitate to attribute so much excellence to Georgia. I have eyewitnesses,[1] I have witnesses by hearsay only who received these things themselves or others had received them from eyewitnesses, which they produced from memory, whose trustworthiness in no way is trifling. And either kind of writer[2] was

---

1. Of these you may refer to that most noble man Phillip George Frederic von Rek, who twice entered the colony and gave a long description about it to us fully with mishaps; then also fully the Reverend men, Johannes Martin Bolzius, and the one who eulogized them to the inhabitants of heaven, Israel Christian Gronav.

2. I have followed six most important commentaries in describing Georgia. First has been ascribed to Samuel Urlsperger: Ausfuhrliche Nachrichten, a Salzburger emigrant into America. Second, das Britísche Reich in America, translated through Theodore Arnold. Third, D. Wilhelm Brest, Predigt vor den Hochanfelhnlichen, Herren Trustees bey ihrer iährlichen Zufammenkunft gehalten 1741 a.d. 18 March; Fourth, D.

so matched, that although their sharp-sightedness and sincerity was not able to be called into doubt, then indeed truly all suspicion of private gain was absent, while they commend this colony with praise. And I add that itself because in all these Georgian affairs it fits wonderfully with it, also they wrote in about many things over a long time and place: that which not at all little made the faith strong to the history of another colony. Those things which I have said about Georgia, I owe especially accepted by writers in the family of the English. Whose writings obviously most accurate about this colony were published. In fact not a few from this race set out daily to this colony; who inform[3] the English about the standing of that colony. But I send these, since with each objection that testimony is made greater, which openly in the public Senate of this colony which sits in the City of Savannah, were confirmed by swearing an oath.

I have nothing more now in wishes and desires than that, kind Reader, this childish attempt, for which my guardian must be praised, which God would wish for a long time for it to be a sound witness!

Ridley Predgit vor den Hochverordneten Herren Trustees abgelegt 1745 6.d. 20 March; Fifth neuefte und richtigfte Nachricht von der Landfchafft Georgia, in which the original account is contained, which was sent to the royal commission for the constitution of this colony; throughout with notes, that the translator put in based on his long residence in America, accompanied by P.M.K. Finally, sixth, allerneuefte Befchreibung der Prouinz Carolina in Weftindien, includes a travel journal of more than a thousand miles among all sorts of Indian nations, translated from the English by M. Vifcher. That author having set out for Carolina in 1700. At which time Georgia was not yet established, but was still joined with Carolina. When he had passed through many thousand miles in a journey through America, he came also into that part of Carolina to which now the name of Georgia is applied; which is apparent he has done brilliantly from the geographical map, which he took care to hammer out.

3. [IN GERMAN] . . . All these things they did first for the purpose of establishing trust of the fortifications which the writers of the Georgia Colony have given us.

He urged me on by his own encouragement, he regarded it just and favorable, and if I have slipped anywhere, may he lift me up by his grace, and also in the future may he be obliging to my studies.

Chapter 1

Since my mind is determined to discuss a few things about the colonies, it seemed to me to explain first the strength and power of this voice. However to me the colony observes closely the region, the large crowd with new inhabitants. So also among ancient tribes in neighboring[1] cities, attacked by the strength of arms, the Romans sent out colonists. In truth in our times Frederick William of most glorious memory, King of Borussia, Salzburgers[2] having been thrown out of their native land because of a confession of evangelical religion, saw to it that a large multitude in parts of his kingdom had to be evicted, then less crowded by men of the time: and so he sent the Salzburgers into a colony. In the same way English Georgia[3] a region of North America, came by the name of a colony. For this was reported by the English as very wild although others had commented[4] about its fertility,[5] as a result it was turned into an English Colony.

---

1. Livy Book 4 chapter 47 and Books 8 chapter 16 agrees.
2. Concerning the emigration of the Salzburgers and their journey into Bornissia, Gekard Gottlieb Gunther has explained brilliantly in the *Emigrations—History* in two volumes.
3. Therefore our colony Georgia must be distinguished from that Asian one which it is agreed has been situated between the Black and the Caspian Sea.
4. Georgia is the part of Carolina turning to the South. In truth Carolina was established by the English, when Charles II, the King of England was ruling. All the way to our times practically the occupants of

About The Excellence of the Georgian English Colony . . .

---

this colony, endowed by royal authority, carried out their rule themselves, until tired of this because of the wars waged with the Indians, they submitted their own rule for a definite sum (fumea) of money to George II, who then when Carolina was changed into an English colony, to the southern part of Carolina, not yet cultivated, he gave the new name of Georgia. The English commentaries of a certain Theodore Arnold, agree concerning all of this consider the account of Theodore Arnold, the English commentary under the title of *British Rule in America* t, I pg. 574 and the following.

 5. See the Allerneueste Nachricht von Georgien, p. 48.

Chapter 2

Because if you are going to believe in the ancient colonies established by the Greeks, the Tyrians, the Romans and the Germans[1] of old; if besides that today's colonies set up by the English, the Batauis, the Spanish, the Lusitanians and many others, you will realize there certainly are a great number of colonies. Therefore if I had to differentiate among the numerous colonies with little figures (figillatim); nevertheless which I perceived first in my mind, to discuss the superiorities of the Georgian-English Colony alone, more sensibly, than which the limits of these pages allow either to measure out its strengths or its space would have to be spread out. Therefore, as I have established my parts I shall explain: I shall set about it in another way, much shorter and easier. First I shall stretch the sinews of my ability in discovering the reasons why colonies were established both in Ancient times and in our times. And at the same time, I shall show as much as I am able. All these reasons, because of which colonies have ever been established came together in Georgia; after that in truth I am going to briefly examine the nature of this colony and its government, as far as it towers above other colonies. I shall point this out very clearly. In truth before I shall begin to discuss this matter: I direct myself very briefly in my paper to search out the first origin of colonies.

---

1. It can be seen in Nicholas Hieronymous Gundlings, *Discours uber die jezigen Staaten von Europen*, t. II, cap. VI, p.3.

Chapter 3

What can be said about colonies established before that time when, except for eight, all men were destroyed by water, we are omitting now. (Noah) Clearly we have no accurate information about that thing. In truth in a difference sense, it is agreed colonies have been sent out from that (time), because[1] all parts of the earth have been settled by human beings, from the foundation of the world to the Flood up to the length of time and the aged life of men, numerous descendants seem to find fault and to conquer. But after the Flood a more accurate description of their origin was given to us by the Holy Spirit. For from these sacred writings it is established,[2] because either in one neighboring generation after the Flood or at least not much after it, colonies already existed in many regions which then possessed the beginnings of cities, republics, and kingdoms.

---

1. Compare the most reverend Sigfried Iacob Baumgarten, translation of the *Allgemeinen Welthistorie*, T. I, p. 223, para.238, who were eager to take away reasoning, before the Flood rained on the following number of men 2,238,030,282,752.

2. There is great division of opinions in what year the division of men took its beginning. Some say that it happened in the first year of the birth of Peleg. Since the name means a division, and was given to him, they say, having been called by an oracle into his own regions as it appears in Gen. 10:25. However that fertile time divided (chronologiam hebraici cedicis) the chronology of the Hebrews from which I hold acts contrary to divine law disappeared in the year 101 after the Flood; from

6   *About The Excellence of the Georgian English Colony* . . .

---

which it must be seen 1AC in the *Origin of Babylon* of Parizoni. Others say Peleg received this name from a physical and geographical division certainly (in parcasm) because at the time of his birth various regions had been cut into parts by the sea, although Peleg signifies the manner, from which then the origin [GREEK WORD] of the Greeks came; in truth, little by little after the flood, men were separated by genealogical division; concerning this thing compare (fume) the sacred chronology of this most revered and very worthy man 10.ALB. Bengeli *The Arrangement of Times*. Others want Sira to be the most ancient kingdom; and Noah himself to be the progenitor of the people of Siren which under the name of (Sahi, Fahi) were venerated up to this point: in truth this opinion has been solidly refuted by the most respected and famous man 1AC. Brucker in (Bistoria) *Criticism of Philosophy* T.4 the second part page 858.

Chapter 4

That custom of sending out colonies then continued among all people. It is established that the Tyrians, Greeks, Carthaginians, Romans and our Germans sent out colonies. The narrowness of these pages, for the literate presentations of those appointed, and space does not permit, that this (book) carry the story of each one of those people about the establishing of colonies, and that we freely call to mind each custom they observed. Finally we shall look more accurately into the purpose of establishing colonies, so that those things which we said in the first place, we shall now accomplish. For who avoids the fact that in almost every action very great movement is the goal? As that fact indicates, does it matter very much if the action is good or bad, undertaken prudently or imprudently, worthy to be praised or cursed? Therefore when all things have been correctly judged, for this reason colonies have been established. I have found four chief causes, the removal as it were of those who were inconvenient rather than helpful to the kingdom; the fruitfulness of the land at a distance which the colonists sought; trade, which takes a big increase from the colonies; and defense from the new colony itself of the kingdom or of the colonies pertaining to the kingdom. In truth we say this is the chief reason, which appears convenient not for private causes but for the public cause of some kingdom. Again it is noted, when a comparison has been made among things of this kind. I have said this is most excellent which either brings more good to the rest, or likewise at the same time embraces those things to which others except in little figures are dedicated. Because therefore if I were to fashion in solid arguments that all these causes one at a time[1] for which each colony has been established came together in Georgia, and it was endowed with many good ordinances, which the other colonies lacked, Georgia was most perfect and surpassed the others. I believe there is no one who would deny on oath.

---

1. The meaning of these words is this: each colony has a chief reason, wherefore it was established, if I investigate the reasons of all the colonies, I shall find these four principles. But not one colony, if you stand back from Georgia, is able to attribute all these to itself at the same time. For one has three, another two, some only one primary cause, wherefore it is established these conditions exist. Only to Georgia alone do those four individual properties exist.

Chapter 5

Therefore among the outstanding reasons for which colonies are established, removal holds first place which is a loss to the kingdom rather than a gain. In truth both because of customs and natural causes men can be a burden to the kingdom. Especially it pertains to natural reasons if the number of the people increases so that the land is not able to produce enough grain to nourish them. Thus Otis,[1] the King of Lydia, when his kingdom was oppressed with a huge famine, he distributed everything having been divided into equal parts by his decree by this plan, those led out by chance, with his son Tofcanian as leader, should look for another region and settle it. In this way they then sought Umbria, called Toscany in our time, and there they were called Tyrrheni after their own leader. Similar reasoning drove the Romans[2] and the Germans of old, that their number having increased too much, they sent colo-

---

1. Namely *Allgemeine Welthistorie* IV Theil p. 630 ¶ 27.
2. Know that Car. Rallins evicts about the Roman colonies in the preface to 1 tom. bift. rom. where among others, these words exist: [THE FOLLOWING TRANSLATED FROM FRENCH] "The multitude of citizens who leave every day from Rome with the new conquests can be charged to this; the colonists observe this inconvenience, and change it into the greatest advantages, and the empire appears stronger. They produce two excellent effects: One, unloading a great number of citizens from the city and for the most part poor; the other guarding the principal (posies) and little by little making the stranger accustomed to Roman habits."

nies into foreign or neighboring lands. Nor did their plan flow from an original theory. For not only was there enough food for the inhabitants left in the kingdom from which they fed themselves, but having set out the colonists subjugated the land, previously uncultivated, with such labor and industry that the harvest responded to their diligence. In truth among moral reasons, because of which men cause disaster to the kingdom, leisure especially must be considered with understanding. In truth in some kingdom where there is a large number of men, there also is a greater crowd of lazy people. In it the crowd consumes the produce of the native born children. There are two kinds of leisurely people; to some whatever way they want the opportunity of preparing food is lacking; many have been accustomed to live by stealing or to beg the nourishment of life from door to door. How much evil is brought in to all republics by those men, especially in our times, some see. For in truth what remedy is able to be applied more eminently to this evil than that men of this kind be sent into colonies? For in colonies is offered to men to whom the opportunity of getting the necessary nourishment is lacking, when they have been given a field to cultivate, from which they may consume bread they have sustenance. In truth those wild people who are fed by stolen or begged-for food after they have been sent into the colonies are able to be forced to work as much as possible by the strength of the laws or punishment. And so those men from which the republic received harm, are able to contribute something to its comfort. But moreover another kind of men exists which is able to stir up many lawsuits in the republic or kingdom in which they live; and it is these who are eager for revolution. In truth in this winding way they are able to increase their own enthusiasm for change; for the most part if they do not hesitate to defend very bitterly with a certain playful tenet with a purer culture and a less suitable religion; especially, if led on certain spurious principles for the most part, if they do not hesitate to defend certain spurious principles very passionately with absolute reverence less consistent with religious ideas. Especially if led on by ambition they aspire to great honors; and if their minds have been set at variance, some resorting to these diversions, others to those divisions. In answer to all men of this type, I say colonies are the best answer. Which indeed I declare as an example from English history it lies hidden from *Tremulis*[3] as they say, led by Penn, Pennsylvania has been stocked. In like manner Virginia[4] and the Barbados[5] were obliged to accept in their own colonies those who because of the English political situation irked their circumstances. For having been chased away and banished, those who took up arms for Charles I, King of England, also all those who were enthusiastic for that rule, were led into jeopardy of life and safety, so that they could not remain in enough safety in England. For this reason they departed into those colonies for the sake of safety. When in truth Charles II had been brought back to his kingdom; those from the opposite side, who before had done things against his father were driven out into those same colonies and fled to those whom they had put to flight before. Therefore many times colonies make a place for deporting those men from a kingdom who bring to a republic or a kingdom more trouble than profit. However, lest anyone should say to us that we only discussed the good things that recommend colonies, and in truth that the evil which some think colonies bring with them we have passed over in silence; we believe those defects which are presented by them also must be discussed.

---

3. See Theodore Arnold's *British Government in America*, t. 11 p. 382.
4. The same, t. 1 p 536.
5. Compare D. Ridley Lord Bischaffs [IN GERMAN].

Chapter 6

There are those who say the riches of a kingdom consist in the large number of inhabitants. Nothing is more harmful to a kingdom or a republic than if the number of inhabitants decreases. We agree with this opinion if every single one of those inhabitants is able to get necessary nourishment for himself in his native soil, and thus contribute something to the common good. However we say no and flatly deny that a great crowd of poor people is a great advantage to any kingdom. Therefore when all the wealth has been left behind in some kingdom, only the poor,[1] to whom the necessities of life were lacking in that same kingdom, migrated into a colony and there we hope to provide great aid for them. The English colonies in America, which are now filled with many thousands of men, were established especially by poor people; now it is all right for many of them to achieve many great riches.[2] If these many thousands of men had remained in England to whom would they have been an asset? But from the colonies they sent back great profits to the English in a sensible way. There is not scarcity of men in England now, is there? Don't the colonies reach out to the kingdom itself? Or don't those who sought colonies remain submissive to the same government? And even when some men set out from other provinces into a strange kingdom and into established

---

1. Compare Gundlings [IN GERMAN].
2. For bringing greater light to this paragraph read [IN GERMAN] where all these are found explained very clearly.

colonies, doesn't their number rather increase through the colonies, who were under the authority of another king? Colonists must not be considered other than free men of the republic. Select testimony exists from that of Livy[3] "what children owe to their parents; those things they (as it were colonists) owe to their parents; those things they (as it were colonists) owe to the Romans, if there is any filial sense of duty, if there is any memory of the ancient fatherland." Therefore those things are increased through colonies, which are in the power and dominion of any king; opportunities are increased; riches are increased. If in truth anyone brings up the fact that the departure of colonists into America made a scarcity of men in Spain; I want him to consider, not only must this be denied, that a great number of people went away into these colonies but yet, when the same danger was about to happen also in other kingdoms which overflow in number of men up to this point; the reasons of the scarcity in Spain indeed must be sought in other things: and indeed first in the amazing number of sacrificing priests, of whom a million[4] are counted in this kingdom. It is not permitted for any of these to have wives through their monastic vows; second in that highest point of inquiry into irregularity, which they call heretical to the dreaded tribunal;[5] by which every day very many at the top are condemned, whatever it forbids, men accepting another religion establish a home for themselves in the kingdom, however that increases the number of men in the other kingdom as much as possible; and in a third point, because it keeps away[6] all born outside of Spain from the American Colonies. For these reasons clearly there is so great a lack of men in Spain, unhealthy and oppressive weather and other reasons especially those produced by nature[7] that I rush to silence.

---

3. Book 27 Chap. 11.
4. Compare [IN GERMAN]
5. Compare [IN GERMAN]
6. Of which mention was made expressly in the edict.
7. [IN GERMAN]

Chapter 7

Therefore colonies attract in many places those men thrown out from some kingdom; those who are more rejected than suitable apply, you will come upon colonies for the purpose of breaking up the excessive number of inhabitants, and then those established because of reasons due to nature; you will even find hidden among those men who were eager with twisted thought for revolution. However there is perhaps one among today's colonies, when you omit Georgia, established especially for this purpose, that those, who when they do not cross over, from where they nourish themselves, are a burden to the kingdom, may have a responsibility there; in truth I would not dare to confirm this. Besides in fact a principle has been made, that they should bring poor people to nourish them, although clearly not especially for their discards to be aided, but therefore, in order for the number of men in the colony to be increased poor people have been led over into the colony. Because in truth if the colony was established for this end, so that poor people could be received there, it is able to be proven with substantial arguments that this reckoning would increase the most noble. For it is permitted to call such a colony a perpetual income for the safety of orphans, (ptoechotrophium) and poor people. Therefore I have insisted for such a long time that this praise is able to be given to Georgia alone among today's colonies although others are continually said to be established for the same reason, nevertheless scarcely would I believe it. In truth continual welfare of the needy has been the first effort of this established colony. This clearly was the destination[1] for the poor people, the very same words of the proclamation[2] taught us, because it was given by those in charge. In truth I suggest that must be brought out by the praises of all, because not only to English poor people was refuge given in that colony but even to those who were driven out[3] from their country because of confession of evangelical religion. This is certainly unusual because as far as I remember, it is able to be said in like manner about no other colony. Because if anyone would wish to present Borussia as an example to us since in that place the Salzburgers were received, also he would wish to present this, I would have this answer. Borussia can be considered either as a kingdom or as a colony. If you look at it as a kingdom, an objection is in no way directed against me; for my discourse is about colonies; if you look at it as a colony, it will be proven from history that Borussia, when first it was settled by men, the beginning had been established by this plan that it would receive at anytime those pushed out from their own country because of religion. I say and confirm that this can be tested in no way. And again it is of value concerning other regions in which it is agreed the Salzburgers were received. I submit that not only the Salzburgers, but all those dedicated to the repeated sacred rites of the evangelicals and pushed out of their native land, applied to Georgia. In truth I shall closely look at the summons of the Salzburgers into Georgia, their ocean crossing, and the beginnings of their dwellings. I shall examine openly one at a time the evidence of divine providence. Wherefore I shall speak not from the thing I believe to be, if about all of these, at least about a few. Finally it will make public that singular kindness by which the governors of the colony of Georgia were accustomed to accept all those who sought the colony.

---

1. Consult Arnold, *Beschreibung des Britischen Reichs in America* p. 657, where the chapter dealing with Georgia begins with this description:
2. Consult the Foreword of the *Ausfürlichen Nachtricht der Salzburgischen Emigranten in Georgien*, p. 5.
3. Of which mention was made expressly in the edict.

Chapter 8

When the English had considered the Salzburgers driven from their country and a great part had marched into Belorussia, at last the governors of the Georgian colony decided among themselves to receive 300 of them into Georgia itself. Therefore they gave letters to a certain member concerning the propagation of knowledge of the society of Christ; indeed they first had been informed of their actions from that emigration. So that because of many great difficulties this undertaking seemed confused to him to whom it had been given; also he worked more to get himself out of it. Since in truth all these difficulties which had been spelled out in detail very often to that same board did not turn it aside in any way from its resolve, so that it stood more and more convinced in it that project was carried out by divine auspices. It was even announced that the Salzburgers would be carried across into England and from there into Georgia at the expense of the governors, and up to that time when they themselves would be able to get crops from their farms, their needs would be supplied from the public granary, and their status would be held in the same manner as that of English citizens, so that, they themselves would rejoice in all those privileges just as the English. And I add that which was promised also from the money of the church was given in interest for these uses for servants, taxes were going to be supplied, so that the Salzburgers ought have no concern about their support. With these promises the governors of the Georgia colony gave to him to whom care had been given for picking the colonists that he should choose the limited number of colonists that he wanted. The society concerning the propagation of the knowledge of Christ gave the same power to him, so that he would choose freely for colonists servants of the divine word pious and wise men and it would send the chosen ones. Because therefore if we trusted this same unexpected and unforeseen invitation, and if we trusted these most suitable conditions publicly confirmed, I think no one would be able to be (who does not look carefully) that the singular providence of God is in the business.

Chapter 9

Therefore after the power was given to send certain Salzburgers to Georgia, in four groups they were sent to that colony. They filled the number of the first crossing with 42 people. These, with God as their leader, set out from Augusta on the 31st day of October 1733. Everywhere on their journey they were welcomed with great joy, and treated with many kindnesses. They arrived safe at Rotterdam on the 27th day of November: near this city interpreters of the divine word were chosen several days before they had landed. The names of the pastors were Balzius and Gronav: one of whom was the assistant inspector of the Latin school of the Halenfis orphanage, the other was the instructor for it. Immediately therefore, they undertook the duty to call upon and to beg for divine help. They boarded the ship the second day of December. Having been much tossed about by the waves, they landed[1] in the English port of Dubrens on the 22nd day of December. The eyes and minds of all were directed toward their arrival. On the journey itself the Salzburgers bore themselves in such an outstanding way that they received the favor[2] of all the English who saw them. Then having

---

1. It is discussed about all of this in the entire *foreword* of the *Ausführlichen Saltzburgischen Nachrichten*, from which these facts were taken.

2. Taken from reading the letters of a certain man who had no connection with the Salzburgers, written from the port of Dubrens, which were found in the *Ausführlichen Saltzburgischen Nachrichten*, T. 1. p. 50,51 "The pleasantness and calm of the Salzburgers in their suffering

yielded to the oath of faith and bound by the oath of loyalty, they began their naval journey on the eighth day of January 1734. With a favorable wind and with God supporting them, they arrived unharmed on the 12th day of March in the largest town of Georgia whose name is Savannah.[3]

---

and the joyful thankfulness with which they carried themselves testify, was so clearly flourishing among them that all present were heartily moved by them. I must recognize that this was a great honor for a Protestant land, and especially Great Britain, that to such regions and realms a migration of such people was made that had left all for the free knowledge of the clear gospel. We also hear that the Salzburg emmigrants perform their prayers publicly every morning and evening, and bear themselves in a most orderly and holy way."

3. About all which happened to the Salzburgers on the journey is written in den Reife—*Diaries of Herren Prediger* T.1. p. 48-82.

Chapter 10

The next year,[1] to be sure 1734, on the 23rd of September again around 50 Salzburgers were sent to Georgia. On the 3rd day of November they arrived in London, where they were adorned with many, indeed the greatest kindnesses, with a certain royal family of Indians[2] they boarded the ship on the 12th day of November, and on the 13th (decimo tertio) of January 1735 safe they were carried to the city of the Salzburgers, called Ebenezer. In 1735 a third[3] group of colonists followed who set out from Augusta of the Vindelici for Georgia on the sixth day of September under divine guidance, they arrived on the 16th of February 1736.

---

1. Compare the Foreword to the *Ausfürlichen Saltzburgischen Nachrichten*, p.17.
2. Compare the previous Foreword, p.33
3. Compare the honorable Philipp George Friedrichs von Reck, his *Reise Diarium*; and the *Ebenezerische Nachrichten*, T.1. Continuation. II, p. 803.

Chapter 11

The fourth[1] departure of Salzburgers into the colony of Georgia was carried out in 1741 in that year, sixty departed for it. At this time no less unusual evidences of divine providence manifested themselves. For, for this group of colonists making their way through the dukedom of Wurtemberg so many supplies had been collected that they almost could not have been larger. Especially by the outstanding, profound plans of the man George S.D.W. the concern which he bore for them is not able to be filled with enough praise. Therefore having set out from Augusta on the 12th day of June, they came to London the 25th of July whence, the ship having set sail the 18th day of September under happy auspices, they arrived on the 21st of December of that same year at the Georgia city Ebenezer.

---

1. Let it be read in the Foreword of the seventh Continuation of the *Ebenezerische Nachrichten*; further in the IX continuation of the Reise-Diarium of the honorable Johannes Gottfried von Mullern, the commissary of this transport up to London, p. 1176. and the *Diarium* of the honoratble Vigera from London to Ebenezer, p. 1205.

Chapter 12

Those three colonies, following the first, sent to Georgia bore themselves no less outstandingly on the journey, so that the Germans, especially in truth the English, received unbelievable pleasure from them. For this reason to be sure many remarkable testimonies exist. But let us return to the first Salzburger colony, and let us consider briefly the reason for its establishment. Then Savannah was the head in those granted regions, they had to spend some space of time there while the location of another city about to be established was chosen. When the location was chosen in a very charming region, they named the city established for the new colony Ebenezer,[1] flowing with a river, blessed of benefits in the remembrance of all from God.

---

1. About this mention was made in the *Reise-Diarium* of the honorable minister, *Salzburger Nachrichten*, T.1, p. 82 etc.

Chapter 13

I think I have shown clearly enough the superiority of Georgia over other colonies, because it held to the first reason for establishing colonies. Therefore I shall proceed to the second, for which it is clear colonies were established. The principal cause we said was the fertility of each colony. Among ancient tribes the Romans are an example to us. Chiefly for this reason they waged such great wars with the Carthaginians about Sicily, since they knew both in peace and in war they needed a very good storehouse of grain.[1] Encouraged by the fertility of the land, the Germans brought in war with the French and Italians. Even today especially for this reason into the most remote regions of the earth colonists have been led to open space. Now I consider it to be my duty to point out the charm and fertility of Georgia which must be considered, equally to establish very clearly in the mind's eye the superiority of this colony above many others. In truth we call the land auspicious both by way of its charm and fertility, to whom these three things have been bestowed by a most benevolent God the parent of all things: that *first* the temperate weather has been considered from whence the heat in summer is not so great because of the shade, so that the inhabitants may almost dry up before the heat nor is the strength of the cold so great in the winter time, so that everything is stiff with ice; *second* that the land has been made ideal both for producing all kinds of fruit and also in other things pertaining to human life;

---

1. See Livy Book 26 Chapter 40 and Book 27 Chap. 5.

there are all kinds of animals, forests and many other things, it pours forth such a supply and abundance that so far it is not necessary for them to seek produce and other things from other kingdoms; rather they themselves can export many things into other regions; *third* finally the air too is healthy, where very few diseases arise. I have discovered this region has these three attributes; I declare it most fertile and charming.

Chapter 14

Indeed the warmer heat is enough for the richness of the land; since it is agreed in these regions, where the heat is so temperate such as in Germany and England there is no harvest of very many fruits most necessary now delights of human life; nothing is grown that you may call sweet or all other kinds of spicy things. In truth where the heat of the sun warms the land a little more, that region brings forth more and better fruits; since indeed the bounty of the land approaches the heat of the sun, as in Italy, where the earth produces many different kinds of fruits which do not ripen in Germany, England, or other regions unless the most diligent pains are taken. Nonetheless however, if the air heats up so much by the warmth of the sun as in lands which are in the line of the equinox, as they say, or near it, or not very far from it, it is consumed by heat, those regions bear very little of all fruits which of these regions do you judge the best location? That one certainly which is between these lands, which we are accustomed to call temperate and those we call burned up. Therefore since almost the last degree of the temperate zone is the 60th and the top of the torrid zone is the first, the 30th degree holds the middle; for that reason we will have that location of the region as the most suitable and propitious for temperate weather. And Georgia lies at this very degree. Besides geographical maps and commentaries[1] about that colony state all

---

1. This description is found in Arnold, Beschreibung des Britischen Reichs in America, T. I, p. 657. It is a large stretch of land, South of Carolina, bordered by the Savannah River, and to the South by the

that region between the 99th and 34th degree lie open. All the regions under those same degrees or in their vicinity carry praise of unusual fertility. In truth for example there are Madera, Cyprus, the very fertile part of Egypt, the Holy Land, the most warlike part of Persia, the most excellent part of China, besides the land of Japan; all of which are not able to be honored with enough praise in travelogues for their fertility and charm. Therefore the degree of heat or of cold which our colony attains is so matched that in practically most months of the year really without interruption[2] in the burning heat, with the northeast wind blowing, the inhabitants always enjoy a charming coolness. Therefore in each month of the year when the settlers would work less in the field, they are held back neither through heat nor cold.[3] How great is the good fortune of this region! The ministers informed us in their own notes of the divine word, because it was spread abroad among the Malabaros that there is as much heat in this land in the winter time as is in our summer days;[4] in truth there is so much glare from the heat of the

---

Alalamacha River, which are both big and terrifying. From one river to the other it is 60 to 70 Miles by sea. And from one side to the other—rest assured (which accounts are more to be believed, as they are more recent) is 120 Miles, (by land, however, Georgia is at least 180 English, or 45 German miles, long, along which it has three levels) and its length from the Sea to the Apalatian or Appalachian mountains is over 300 miles, and as it goes from the sea it gets wider and broader.

2. Compare, *Neueste Nachricht von Georgien*, p. 32, *Ebenezer Nachrichten*, T. I, p. 2394, under the date of the 24th of July. "The heat is so temperate that our happy people could not wish for a better climate for their labors after they, little by little, became accustomed to it. They can work in the fields winter and summer and their livestock can be let loose in the fields all year, which are two great advantages."

3. Compare *Ebenezer Nachrichten*, T. II, p. 64. People in Germany can work little or not at all in the fields during winter, while in this place, the wintertime is almost the most comfortable for work in the fields.

4. See Nickamps, *Kurzgefasste Missions Geschicht*, p. 30 and 31.

sun especially in the hours of the middle of the day that the eyes cannot be opened without pain. Therefore isn't this region so blessed that it rejoices in the controlled heat of the sun? Therefore it is evident by its own accord that Georgia must be preferred to all the Asiatic colonies near the line of the equinox or placed in its vicinity, as Java, Sumatra Ceylon, Borneo, the Moluccan and the Philippine Islands, besides Guinea in Africa the islands of S. Laurentia, truly it is superior to Hispaniola in America, New Spain, the islands of Barbados and others. Besides all these, in considering the favorable weather of the region Georgia must be preferred to those colonies in which the force of the cold in wintertime is a little sharper as Pennsylvania, Virginia and others.

Chapter 15

Now also another matter must be considered and discussed concerning Georgia because it is so placed in the fruitfulness of the region that at first it would bring forth abundantly all fruits, then other things pertaining to human life where naturally animals and shady meadows are concerned and that people would produce other things certainly with no slacking off. Thus in truth I am drawing up my reasons concerning the very rich harvest of all produce: whatever region has heat and this kind of weather so that on either side it is suitable for bearing all produce, that colony is able to produce all crops; and in fact I can report all this about Georgia. That which now I shall affirm in solid arguments, the following will shed greater light on all of it. Georgia by the benefit of its heat can produce those things which are grown in the most torrid lands. Rice is produced from the land in almost all regions near the line of the equinox, as a matter of fact, in those places where practically nothing else is able to grow because of the great heat of the sun; however in Georgia it is produced abundantly.[1] Wherefore do not be amazed that all things which are produced from the land in Jamaica[2] and Barbados, where the heat of the sun is lower, such as

---

1. See *Ebenezerische Nachrichten* T. II, p. 46, p. 63.
2. Compare the sermon delivered by The Lord Bishop of Glouchester, D. Riedley. Before the Lord Trustees in the year 1745, further in the *NeuesteNachricht von Georgien*, p. 34, and 38, and also *Ebenezer Nachricht*, T. I, p. 183.

sugar, pepper, coffee, pineapples,[3] ginger, citrus, splendid golden apples, trees which they call coco and also cacao,[4] besides tobacco, indigo shell fish,[5] cinnamon and many other things are similarly produced from the earth in Georgia. For this reason you will not rashly conclude that work would certainly not be useless, concerning producing the rest of the spices even if there were danger. Indeed those crops are produced in Georgia for which only a temperate degree of heat is needed. Among these wine holds first place. The first colonists of Georgia, who arrived in this region found large grapes of pleasing flavor and charming sweetness growing

---

3. Pineapples grow to the size of a lemon or a melon, they taste so noble, like strawberries, apples, peaches, quince, grapes cherries, apricots, sugar, honey and Rhinewine, and they still have a special unique taste that one can hardly describe, because of which they are also, because of their splendid taste and fragrance, called the king of fruits and are preferred to all others. Iohannes Geoge Nicola Dieterichs. *Phytanthozoiconographia*, under the heading, pineapples.

4. Compare the cacao, a tree of middling size, the inner seed of which is needed for chocolate, and whose oil is especially good for health. Idem, T.II, under the head Cacao.

5. Arnold, T. II, p. 1192. The cochineal, or scarlet berry comes from a fruit called the gooseberry (or Indian fig); it bears a leaf with a mucousy property and a fruit, that is blood-red and full of seeds; the insect, however, which feeds on the fruit and flowers produces a strong and lasting color. It appears first as a small paleness or button on the leaves of the bush, on which they are produced, which later, through the heat of the sun, becomes a living insect, little vermin or worm. These worms become flies in time and (prepare themselves for a long journey) thus one may, with steam from burning stuff, drive them from the bushes where the insects get their nourishment, whence the insects are smothered and killed, so that when one shakes a plant, they fall onto a cloth and thus with little effort a great quantity can be collected.

wild,[6] anticipating evidence[7] of very sweet wine at some time or other. Therefore a test was undertaken, after in fact vine sprouts from the island of Madera[8] were brought in and ingrafted in Georgia earth; the wine sprouted from such good stock because it was certainly not inferior to the Madera. Also Mulberry trees[9] bearing both white and red varieties, which are most pleasing flavor, are found there in huge numbers. Leaves even furnish food for silkworms. Whence no vain hope shines forth that a most profitable trade will be established at some time in Georgia[10] nor must the

---

6. *Ebenezer Nachrichten*, T. I, p. 378, under the date of 25 July. "Some of us obtained a great quantity of grapes in the country, the berries from which was of such great quantity and strong taste that one soon felt the force of it in one's head."

7. See *Ebenezer Nachrichten*, T. II, p. 906. This is according to the opinion of those who understand such things, a striking land; of which the Germans in Savannah can hardly say enough in their letter about how noble a wine region this is. L.c.p. p.2213. If one wished to come here with grape stock, one could harvest grapes twice in one year from each vine, which the Lord General Oglethorpe's vinyardist has shown for two years.

8. See; Neueste *Nachrichten* von Georgien, p. 34. As to which sorts of vine flourish best here, especially Malvefier and Madiera vines, from which island shoots have be brought to Georgia, and with which province Georgia is in very much the same latitude. See, Ebenezerische Nachr. T. II, p.905.

9. Compare l.c. p. 856.

10. See Arnold, T. I, p. 675. Where these words are found: "Concerning the last (namely Mulberry trees) will make for the best growth of the silkworm, they eat it, and the hope, which those, that live in them, and us, as we prefer a house, created from that. Two or three Piedmontese came with the first ship to teach people the way one should work with silkworms, the eggs of which someone brought from Italy, and they soon developed into a packet of worms, that were sent to the house of Thomas Lombard for testing, which goods he tested with his instruments for strength and said of it: the silk of Georgia is the best silk to work that I have ever seen, even better than our best, superfine Piedmont, and it

harvest of[11] the cotton plant which is abundant in this colony be belittled. Many kinds of fruit trees,[12] as for example there are apples,[13] pears,[14] cherries, the very best in persian[15] fig trees, Cretan apples (quince), hazel nuts, chestnut trees, almond trees, plum trees,[16] and all other fruits, originating in Italy, to which especially you may add the olive,[17] no less bless Georgia with a very abundant harvest. But not only in these fruits which desire the more intense and more gentle heat of the sun; but also those which have need of such temperate heat as in our lands, Georgia produces; in the number of which you may reckon wheat,[18] spelt,[19] barley,[20]

---

proved itself immensely good in uses and tests it has undergone. Now that we have proved the value of its properties." The English author continued, "so we have only to hope that we can produce it in greater quantity, which can't happen so long as hands are lacking who can help increase food and the comforts of life."

11. See *Ebenezerische Nachrichten*, T. II. p. 399 182 Many people in our area have planted cotton, some more, others less, which they, stockings made of which are expensive, have enriched.

12. Ebenezerische Nachrichten, T. II. p. 933.

13. l.c. p. 873.

14. l.c. p. 1075.

15. We have many sorts of figs, all of the most agreeable taste.

16. l.c. p. 514.

17. l.c. p. 1856.

18. l.c. p. 1856. 1856 in a letter written 13 May 1742, Tome II p. 1235. These words stand out: finally our people gathered their wheat, some before and some after Christmas. And one could not see this success without pleasure and love of the God of orphans.

19. l.c. p. 1103. I have now new confirmation that the best fully-worked land produces not just a hundredtimes, but a thousand time, which would otherwise be almost unbelievable. From 3 kernels of rye in time from the earth, one woman has obtained a little sack completely full of kernels. From a single kernel 170 good ears grew; it was similar for wheat, barley and oats.

20. l.c. p. 1929. The growth in this hot land produces altogether more seed than in Europe. The Rye, Barley and Oats is as good as in Europe, but produces very richly.

oats, hemp, flax, indian[21] grains and all kinds of pulses,[22] besides turnips,[23] cucumbers and vegetables of different kinds. I am omitting hyssop (herb of mint family) and other medicinal herbs, clearly unknown[24] to us which the region itself brings forth of its own accord abundantly.

---

21. *Ebenezerische Nachrichten* T. I p. 842. Indian corn grows like Turkish wheat in big stems. One places about 5 or 6 kernels in a hole. Each hole is at least a good step from the next; between each plant of corn are planted Indian beans or peas, so that the corn stalks serve the vine, and the pease, with their vines, hold the corn together so that the wind cannot pull it down so easily. On each stalk of corn are 2 or 3 ears, and each ear has 100, 2, 3, 4 or 5 hundred kernels.
22. *Ebenezerische Nachrichten* T. II p. 2037, 2058.
23. *Ebenezerische Nachrichten* T. I p. 373.
24. As they are. e.g. Mytel thus; this herb produces green berries that, when cooked, make green wax, of which one makes candles. From 2 rakings one gets about 25 pounds. There is also a grass, called silkgrass, which is very long and strong so that one can use it as a rope; and an Indian pepper, that is very strong and hot. Mayapple, the fruit of which is very pleasant to eat, potatoes, a sort of West-Indian potato (earth-apple), is so sweet, firm and when it is baked in coals can be used in the place of bread. P. 841 & 42. Squashes who's taste is much like that of green tea. p.852. Much is said of all this in the Newest Description of the Province of Carolina in the West-Indies, translated from the English by M. Vischer.

Chapter 16

I think I have demonstrated enough the first part of my premise that Georgia is able to bring forth all kinds of produce namely with the help of its heat and now will bring forth many more. Although in truth the heat not only pertains to growing fruits of all kinds but also the fertility of the land does a great deal for that; I shall enumerate certain things about the fruitfulness of the soil. In almost all places the land is flat near the shore: but yet when you go back a little more from the shore, you will find it a little more hilly[1]

---

1. *Ebenezerische Nachrichten* T. II p. 1141. A certain potter, on orders from Lord. General Oglethorpe traveled among the Indians around the town, and he has seen all sorts of curious things, in part with his own eyes and in part [learned of them] from credible persons. He told me, among other things that he found among the Tzericky [Cherokee?] Indians a small mountain where, among the rocks, the footprints of a very swift people, namely many men women and children with all sorts of poultry, birds and beasts are to be seen. One can also see the shape of a man fallen on the ground, which is lifting itself back up with both hands, so the backside and heels marked in the stone are seen just as if they were in the sand. I believe the account of this upright man as surely as if I had seen it. The Indians themselves know almost all there is to say of it. There is also in the same area a fire-belching mountain. Thus a great cave in the cliff, from which a certain material spews constantly, and when it falls to ground it turns to rock. There are many deep cliff caves, just as in Canaan. He didn't learn enough of the fertility of this area to describe it.

but more fertile. In many places it is so gentle and mild, that it is not necessary for the inhabitants either with horses or oxen to break it up with a plow.[2] Because if they were to do that by hand, they would restore the cultivation of the soil more easily.[3] In truth four[4] kinds of earth are discovered in Georgia. That soil in which pine trees are found is sandy; where there are oak trees, it is fertile and suitable for many kinds of grain; where there are lakes, there is the greatest fertility of the fields, where that kind of meadow which they call Savannah is found, it is especially suitable for grazing and pasture lands. Besides this the region is widely irrigated by many rivers,[5] lakes, brooks, and fountains whose water is pleasant and sweet. Nobody in Georgia changes his [LATIN WORD] (vitium) because the kinds of land are so diverse it rather renders that soil which is suitable for any crops he wishes to raise.[6] For all kinds of produce do not require rich soil, but some sandy, others swampy, and still others grassy. There are those which love shade, others

---

2. *Ebenezerische Nachrichten* T. I p. 223.
3. *Ebenezerische Nachrichten* T. II p. 2210.
4. See the *Britische Reich in America* T. I. p. 673.
5. *Ebenezerische Nachrichten* T. 1 p. 81; *Allerneueste Beschreibung der Provinz Carolina in the year 1700* p. 71. About 30 Miles up the Savannah River we reached the fruitful Gostade of the Saponna (or Savannah) River. All of Europe has no river so pleasing, if only Christ comes to it and it is through intelligent preparations developed. This lovely river is a bit broader that the Thames in England near Kingston, and contained through its dazzling marble cliffs, it has a steady, graceful flow. A flock of swans and other waterfowl swim there, so uncommon that the eye stays fixed on them. In front of the spring perch birds with nests and they sing, so that there is a growing echo to the lovely hills. The one side of the river is bordered by a rough soil, the other is so fruitful that one is constantly reminded of the West Indies.
6. See: *Britische Reich in America* p. 673 where these words can be read: "It is truly a good proportion of these 4 sorts of lands, and as the land gets higher, the soil gets better. Men have found this soil to the suitable for all sorts of English crops and for most English fruit trees.

mountains, some even love valleys: therefore Georgia is able to supply whatever location is especially desirable. Wherefore by right and merit the conclusion is permitted that Georgia[7] is most suitable for producing all kinds of crops by reason of its heat and of the land itself.

---

7. See: *Ebenezerische Nachrichten* T. I p. 179 in the Lord of Reck's description of Georgia these words can be read, "And because the land of Georgia is comfortable and fruitful, it can be made as beautiful and useful as the best of current colonies in a short time if a proper number of workers are employed."

Chapter 17

Since in truth it is not sufficient in human life that the very fertile earth produce all crops; but it is even required that also an abundance of other things pertaining to human life be made; right now I shall point out what has been prepared concerning Georgia for their inspection. First among them must be considered the living kingdom, as they say. Animals in truth are accustomed to be divided into five classes. First quadrupeds both those tame and wild; then winged creatures, further on aquatic creatures; besides reptile, and finally amphibians. In reviewing these five classes, I shall run over the animals by species that are found in Georgia. Therefore bear in mind about tame animals that so great a variety of them has been brought over from Carolina into Georgia that there is no species that is not maintained there and found in abundance. Since they are able to use the pastures in all months of the year, they grow fat; especially it produces sheep and hogs, they bring forth multiple breeding. In truth especially the horses, who are of proven fertility, offer great hope of establishing stables. But a farm in Georgia is not lacking in wild animals. For there is found a large supply of deer, young bucks, wild goats, elk, buffalo, bears, beavers, hares, rabbits, mountain goats, and squirrels. Beasts eager for plunder and carnivorous animals which have their dens and home there are panthers, cats[1] lingering in the mountains, similar

---

1. *Ebenezerische Nachrichten* T. II p. 2248. Moreover, more of this in Allerneuesten Nachricht von Carolina.

in nature and size to panthers, wild cats yet of small size; further on tigers which in fact are rarely seen, wolves, foxes, musky smelling dormice which supply the best moss. With flying animals must be counted eagles, pelicans,[2] Indian roosters,[3] pheasants, woodcocks, plain partridges, wild doves, all of which there is a huge supply: also turtledoves, parrots, blackheaded snipes, larks, swans; you will kill these in the wild along with many others whose names[4] now escape us. No less do the Georgians abound in a rich supply of fish. For since the territory of Georgia is by the sea, all kinds of saltwater fish are found there. Always very many rivers wind in their course through this region which team with fish,[5] also a huge number of streams are found there whose names would be long to list.[6] To the reptiles certainly you will add the snakes;[7] among the amphibians in truth you will include the crocodile and also that which is named alligator.[8]

---

2. *Ebenezerische Nachrichten* T. 1 p. 894 The pelican is almost as big as a goose. Its beak is 2 inches wide and 17 long. It has a big sack under the lower half in which it collects mussels, which it keeps until they open, then it spits them out again and picks out the flesh. It flies heavily and slowly and lives on fish. It is a fable that it cuts its breast and gives the blood to its young.

3. *Ebenezerische Nachrichten* T. I. p. 857.

4. E.G. Racoon [possum]. It is a sort of Indian dog and has on its underside a sack in which it carries its young from one place to another. Its flesh is like that of a suckling pig.

5. *Ebenezerische Nachrichten* T. I. p. 2319 & T. II. p. 874.

6. A more complete description of all these is found in *Ebenezerische Nachrichten* and *Neuesten Nachricht von Georgien*; auch *Neusten Nachricht von Carolina*.

7. *Ebenezerische Nachrichten* T. I. p. 182 & *Allerneuste Nachricht von Carolina*, p.200 et seq.

8. *Ebenezerische Nachrichten*. T. 1 839 The alligator is an amphibian of 16, 17, 20 and more feet long, almost like a crocodile. The flesh reeks strongly of musk, especially 4 stones or glands, which one can pulverize and use as a medicine for dropsey. It is said that in the fall the alligator swallows a single nut, which gives him food for the entire winter.

Chapter 18

The forests hold the second place among those things which are necessary for human beings. Now indeed I shall not discuss their usefulness which is very great, since that has been made clear: the soil will help explain those things which pertain to Georgia. Certainly the commentaries give us the following description of them. The woods with which Georgia is filled are crowded with trees all of which are most suitable for building and burning. They are found to be tall and rarely crooked. First among these are the oaks whose wood which skilled carpenters use without a doubt surpasses the others in the whole of America. Among these are also nut trees which furnish the best wood for iron workers, next the cedars,[1] red and white cypress,[2] quince, laurels, alder trees, white cinnamon wood pines which they use for making masts; besides trees called sassafras[3] whose wood and flowers are highly praised

---

1. l.c. p. 243. This night we camped on a deserted cedar island. Ebenez. T. II, p. 2154 this cedar wood is streaked a beautiful red and white with lovely smelling wood that lasts for a long time.

2. l.c. p. 2145. Cypress wood is generally found in marshy and watery areas. Of unusual thickness and height, which is very soft and workable and long lasting wood which is very useful for canoes and building.

3. l.c. p. 809. Many large and small sassafras trees grow in the area, which produce a truly pleasant smell. We're certain that one could dry it and use it in the place of tea, and it might have the advantage over the usual East Indian tea. We have gathered some and will make a test.

for use in purging the blood. Beech trees, poplars, myrtles, ash trees, fir trees, birch, willows, with many others[4] whose names I now allow to be concealed, grow happily in Georgia. Next there are many kinds of reeds; and in the forests incredible armies of bees: whence great quantities of honey[5] and wax flow into the colony.

---

4. It is read: *Allerneuste Nachricht von Carolina*.

5. On all of this see *Allerneuste Nachricht von Carolina*, the *Beschreibung des Britischen Reichs* offers this description of the southern part of the British colony of Carolina, of which Georgia was a part: "In all parts of Carolina the wind is so moderate and the seasons so orderly, that it is not clear whether the cold or the heat is better. Although there is a sort of winter every year; it is altogether so unremarkable, that one is hardly aware of it. The pleasant moderation is caused by the wind, that the banks of the river are covered with all sorts of healthy trees; and many such have grown nearby, and so provide the eye with a thousand so beautiful and varied landscapes, that the pleasure is equal to being enchanted. In most places near the river the ground is difficult, but it becomes, bit by bit, higher, with little mountains, that lie in a fruitful plateau, that are also covered in flowers. Under these mountains are wonderful valleys, covered in herbs and a nearby spring, from which rushes a refreshing spring. There are many thick shrubs, among which all sorts of useful herbs grow. The Indians use these to treat sicknesses. There is sasparilla, Asian rush (cane), cichle, and resin, which is very good for wounds and bruises, and such an amazing quantity of Honey, which the bees make everywhere, that the supply is unending. From this one makes a liquor and a mead that is as good as dry Malaga. The bees swarm 5 or 6 times. There is a tree from which an oil flows that has an extraordinary ability to heal wounds; and another tree that gives a balsam very close to the balsam of Mecca.

Chapter 19

Now we have said concerning the fertility of Georgia how much crops, fruit and produce one beholds: these things necessarily pertain to a very fertile region since they contribute a great deal to sustaining human life. But there are other things which if they are found in a certain region indeed must not be considered of little value indeed, in truth, if they are absent, they can be reported too little among the colony's faults. Among these I name gold, silver, and other metals, next gems and pearls. I declare by all law these are not considered to be among the necessary requirements of a very fertile land, but they cannot be lacking to it. For the region which abounds in fruit and other things not only furnishes food lavishly to its inhabitants, but also produces grain for sale, and is able to acquire a huge amount of gold and silver for itself by this trade. In truth where the greatest fruitfulness of the region from mining is sought, there the inhabitants perish from hunger unless grain is brought in from other places by means of much gold and silver. England[1] and Batavia lack mining of gold and silver, but yet they are far wealthier than Germany and Hungary because they distribute agricultural products. Therefore although Georgia has been made most suitable for carrying on trade; that is considered in a lower place for many, however, if it should be lacking in gold, it will offset that by abundant trading. But what answer to many of all

---

1. Gundlings. *Discours über die Europaeische Staaten.* T. I cap. IV. Para 35, p.618.

48   *About The Excellence of the Georgian English Colony . . .*

these? There are indications[2] that Georgia is not totally empty of gold especially, silver, and other metals, also gems particularly pearls. Thus also the Georgians say that they have found marble[3] and a certain kind of earth from which porcelain, believing very little[4] china, is able to be made hard. No less fuller's[5] earth is found there beyond the chance of a doubt.

---

2. *Neueste Nachricht von Georgien.* p. 38 and *Allerneueste Nachricht von Carolina* p. 310 Silver and other metal-mining are being pursued. We are delighted with them, and they are very rich in Carolina and the surrounding areas, of which the Indians have known for a long time, but they do not dig for it, except when the hidden ore shows itself at the surface.

3. *Allerneueste Beschreibung von Carolina.* We spent this day on a large tract of land. Today a very good marble is discovered, and it extends for more or less 500 English miles. The land increases in marble and fruitful soil. At midday we rest and have our mealtime on a marble stone, of which towers halfway out of the ground and might be a part of the orient. It was very flat with here and there little red berries, like Lachs-Roegen. And strong springs of healthy waters rise out of the big stones, from which I have often drunk on my journeys. This area also produces good stone for buildings of many kinds.

4. *Ebenezer Nachricht.* T. II. p. 1148. A potter in Savannah has come upon the art of making Chinese ware or porcelain. He also knows of a place in this area a marble- stone of which he has made some tests. Of which he asserted an intention, there should be work for around one-hundred men on the land and river.

5. *Allerneueste Nachricht von Carolina*, p. 47 We slept this night by a brook, where I myself came across a gossamer gold earth, just like Brussels sand, which goldsmiths need, and in England and other places is accounted more expensive [than gold]. One also finds the true blood-stone, near an considerable fuller's earth that I tested on a large stain on a woolen garment, and found it very good. See Gundlings, *Discours über die Europaeische Staaten.* T. L. Can IV para. 47 p. 644.

Chapter 20

Actually you should not wonder at the great fertility of Georgia, since all those crops in those land's which are placed under the same degrees (latitude) you will find in Georgia. For the best Madera wines the yield of Shiraz[1] of China are harvested under the same degrees of latitude. Oil, cotton, grains, wheat, barley and rice are the common[2] products of almost all lands situated under these latitudes. Therefore do not wonder that Georgia enjoys the

---

1. *Allg. Welthistorie* T. IV p. 71 in the notes. The wine know as Shiraz is a very strong wine that is so strong that one can, without diminishing the taste, mix with two parts of water. Cong. I. G. Worms. East Indian and Persian Travels. p. 262.

2. Argensola gives us this description of the Chinese empire in Lib. IV of The Moluccan Islands p. 461-464. Most of the land is very temperate and has a beautiful and broad hill, a healthy wind, and the sun is very rarely covered by mists. It happens that the earth is very fruitful, and many years two or three plantings can be made. In the villages and towns one finds woods and vineyards; the fields are full of rice, barley and various grains and things useful to human life. There are also all sorts of birds, many wild game, great seas, groves and forests, gold, silver, iron and other ores, pearls and precious stones, porcelain, that cannot be copied, beautiful furs against the cold, silk and wool, cotton, linen, sugar, amber and musk, of which Greek and Latin authors didn't write, are as common in China as in any other place in the world. Similarly, Persia agrees best with our Georgia, of which much is said in the same World History T. IV p. 77-88.

same crops, as those very lands because its fertility is not any less than theirs for this purpose, and the heat of the sun is the same in it, because indeed it produces the same minerals, which they produce. In truth it is known that so great a supply of gold and silver is in China, Japan[3] and Chile[4] that there is scarcely any in all the other kingdoms. Persia abounds with pearls, and in fact the island of Ormus[5] which is very near in the 29th degree of latitude produces a huge supply of them. Also for the same reason the land of Georgia is seen most suitable for producing porcelain, a little after China. Indeed you may ask about Thea and I shall explain everything shortly: Georgia is a region of this kind, which has been provided and adorned with every dowry by nature, blessings which God has attributed to the most auspicious lands. For indeed when Israel[6] gave the greatest blessings to his sons, among which was also fertility of the land, he stood before their eyes and said "Jehovah, your God, will lead you to stay in a good land, a land of waters, rivers, and fountains and lakes flowing now through valleys and now through mountains; a land of wheat and barley, vines, fig trees, pomegranates, a land of olive trees and abounding in honey; a land in which you will eat your food without lack, nor will you be in need of anything: a land whose rocks are iron, and from whose mountains you will dig metals" Deut. 8: 8-10. This description of

---

3. Conf. N. H. Gundling T. 1, c.III para. 29 p. 445. In Japan silver is more valuable than gold, and one gets gold with as much difficulty as one acquires silver.

4. conf. Gundling T. I p. 139 In the city of Potosi, in Chile, there is a great silver mine, from which Spain has already taken 3500 million. Chile has pearl fisheries, equal to those of the pearl islands, that appear near all piles of clam. There is also an emerald ground, where one finds many emerald mines.

5. *Allgemeine Welt-Historie*. T. IV, p.76.

6. Deut. VIII. v. 8,9,10.

a very fertile land coincides most accurately with our Georgia;[7] and nothing more must be desired, than that the inhabitants of this land compose all their lives according to the divine rules which are held totally in this summary: for thus the Israelites having been made participants themselves by the divine gift of this same promised blessing, were rich in an abundance of all things.

---

7. Earlier we revealed clearly enough the testimonies concerning the fertility of Georgia: from this I do not believe there it is too much, however if only I may add a few things for the purpose of strengthening that assertion. Such, e.g. are discovered in the *Ebenezer Nachrichten*, T. II, p. 1105. ": It is a place where almost everything grows and livestock also do well. It is easy to make hay, for the best grass grows where crops have stood, really astonishingly, and in time the inhabitants take in the load." In another place. p. 1863. "One can scarcely sow German seed so thinly, that it is not soon thick in this land, that is how rich the soil is. A single seed will become a great bush, green with branches and leaves." And on p. 15, "under the date of February 6, by this date in the so-called spring weather, the trees have broken out and stand beautiful in full bloom. We have become accustomed to the land, it is more pleasing to the Salzbergers than their former fatherland. They can work in the fields the winter through and it is convenient that one can move everything from one place to another on water."

Chapter 21

We proceed to the third requirement of very fertile and charming regions which rests in the soundness and purity of the air. Air becomes unhealthy chiefly in sulfur and other nocuous vapors that are exhaled from the land, which unless they are dispelled by the wind, produce much illness. Very often the heat itself of the sun is as destructive as possible to the human body. Sometimes impure or salty water and fruits harmful to health launch an array of diseases in a certain region. But none of these evils annoy Georgia. For both the violent attack of the winds[1] which often arise in this colony, immediately cleanse the air from impure particles, and the water[2] is so healthy and sweet that it is able to be of very little danger to health. What must be suggested concerning the heat of the sun, has already been shown in a former place; it is absent so much that the climate has not been made friendly to the nature of the body so that rather it does not feel the fury of the sun too much in summer, nor the cold too much in the winter time. I do not say that human beings in this colony are clearly liable to diseases, when the condition of the body is very weak for a person: where, I ask,

---

1. E.g. in *Ebenezerischen Nachrichten*, T. II, p. 12, 41, 112,444, 572, etc.
2. E.g. *Ebenezerischen Nachrichten*. T. II p. 75 where these words are found. "the spring at the orphanage is very deep, and the water from it very fresh, clear and good tasting. and people come to drink from it very happily (it may also be used to brew a thin beer.)"

will you find a region of this kind in which the body of human beings is not afflicted by diseases? It has been asserted in this way, no kinds of diseases prowl around in this colony which the circumstances of the region and the weather engender. Because many colonies were established in the beginning of sickness which in later years would thin out the colonists; thence it chiefly came about because the colonists did not yet understand the nature of the climate. For either worn out by too much justified work, they drank more water, since wine and beer were lacking whence not a few of them were broken and debilitated; or unprepared with enough blankets, they were not able to defend themselves from the cold at night since in Georgia equally, as in all hot regions, the nights, having a relation to the heat of the day, can be called cold: whence rapid and quivering fevers besides diarrhea arise. Also the absence of doctors, obviously they lacked them in the beginning, rendered trivial diseases more dangerous, since the inhabitants had not been instructed with suitable remedies or utterly with none at all. Not only now is healing applied to these ills, but in the future, when everything in our colony will be reported better, greater healing will be added; therefore I think no one is going to deny that Georgia is very healthful.

Chapter 22

Thus, I think, it will be clear that the three qualities which pertain to a most charming and fertile land are rightly attributed to Georgia. Therefore nothing remains than that also I should prove almost no other colony is able by equal right to assume these things for itself. But both time and the space of these pages do not permit me to expand so widely. Therefore I leave this to the kind inquiry of the reader. Meanwhile however in certain colonies the truth of my claim must be shown, that there be in place of proof, what way I wish the other colonies to be examined. How Georgia excels very many colonies in the mildness of its climate has been demonstrated above in Chapter 13. How it is outstanding in the abundance and healthiness of the remaining air, even now I shall explain. So many colonies are depressed by a lack of grain, as Madeira,[1] Jamaica,[2] the Barbados, and the Moluccan islands[3] which produce almost nothing else except dates and spices. Next all those regions in which

---

1. Iacobus Christopher Iselins. *Historical Lexicon*, under Madera: Wine and fruit trees grow plentifully, of grains however very little, so they are most often shipped there from France or Tenerife.
2. *Britisches Reich in America*. Preface: If, however, New England and the other English colonies provide the sugar islands (Jamaica and Barbados) with necessities, and without such they cannot survive, as they know from experience, so it is good enough that they make a return to England of that degree.
3. Bartholomaeus Leonhardus Agensola Libr. 1 de *Insulis Moluccas* p. 29.

56 *About The Excellence of the Georgian English Colony* . . .

there is too much heat and sun are suitable for producing neither wine nor olive trees. You will say the same thing about these places where the heat of the sun is too moderate: therefore in many colonies these things cannot be planted,[4] still they will obtain first place among fluids if you withdraw them from water. For although they bring forth a kind of grape nevertheless they produce wine of a harsh and inconstant flavor,[5] nor do they produce every year, so that there is no effort to squeeze them. Some labor with a lack of wood[6] as the cape of Good Hope, others with a lack of horned cattle[7] as Chile; some are upset by severe earthquakes as Cylanus,[8] Amboina (Malay),[9] the islands of Banda (Indonesia),[10] and Ternate (Indonesia)[11] and Peru.[12] Others are very harmful to health as the Moluccan Islands,[13] Sumatra,[14] Borneo,[15] Makassar Strait (Indo-

---

4. Bielers. *Phytanthozoiconographia*. Under the heading, vitis.
5. Iohannes Gottlieb Worms. *Ostindianische und Persianische Reisen*, p.75.
6. Idem p. 1112.
7. Freizer. *Journey to the South Seas*, ch. XI.
8. Argensola. *De Insulis Moluccis*. Lib. V.
9. Idem lib. XV, p. 1489.
10. Idem lib. XV, p. 1558
11. Idem lib. XII, p. 1234.
12. Of which the most recent examples remain.
13. Argensola, lib. I.
14. Worms, *Ostindianische Reisen*, p. 312: The island of Sumatra is one of the biggest islands of the Indies, but Banda and Ambon because of their poisons and hot climates are the most unhealthy and can, thus, with right be better called the pest coast than the west coast.
15. Idem p. 390. Because the soil is covered with a thin paste or mud, which is baked by the sun, it results in a horrifying, stinking mist, which produces an unbearable stench of the dead frogs and other vermin that stay up on the land and die. The gold, and the abundance of precious stones that lay all around made us unwilling to give up our venture, be the danger never so great.

Chapter 22

nesia),[16] or the Celebes (Indonesia), Ternate (Indonesia),[17] Jamaica,[18] Hispaniola and others. If you will consider how correctly all those things which pertain to a happy scheme of human life (a thing which truly is not able to be done in a correct manner very often, since the history books worthy enough of confidence, and struggling with correct proof are lacking), you will discover a certain particular fault in every single colony; to such an extent Georgia is superior to the other colonies in consideration of its charm.

---

16. Idem p. 429.

17. idem. p.601. The high mountain, of 360 Ruthen (about 3.7 meters/Ruthen) in the middle of the island of Ternate is seen for a long way, and reaches the clouds with its fiery peak. The spray of ash and glowing coals the size of big stones have often rained down on Ambon, 40 miles away. It has at times so poisoned the air, that countless men have died.

18. *Ebenezerische Nachrichten* T.I. p. 163. A certain merchant who stayed in the colony for a while gave this, among many other descriptions: The Island of Jamaica is one of England's richest. The way of life and the great heat in Jamaica, however, damaged men's health, body, soul and life. So sensible men, once they had made something, in time went back. He has a mind to leave so that he will not continue in torment for fear of death and to extend his life in comfort in a place where the air is healthy.

Chapter 23

Trade and wealth which flow from them to the inhabitants are a fourth influence.

Why colonies have especially been established I will not praise the use of trade very much:[1] since it has been made clear and established enough by experience, the best digging of gold and silver is commerce. Because in truth profit itself coming from trade holds to this: that in the very least if many things from foreign lands remain at a high price, merchants will import something desired into the

---

1. The very beautiful words of Rollins about the greatest use of trade are found in volume 7 of Ancient History pg. 377. One can say, without fear of being suspected of exaggeration that trade is the most solid foundation of civilized society, and the most necessary bond for unity between all men of several countries and of several conditions which they make. For in one way, the whole world is not conscious of its own sterility. All its needs are brought to it from a point called the end of the universe, and each region is astonished to find itself burdened with strange fruits which its own ground cannot grow for it, and enriched with a thousand commodities which were unknown to it, which nevertheless bear the sweetness of life. It is by trade of the sea and rivers, that is to say by navigation, which God one among, all men in a manner so marvelous taught them to conduct and govern the two most violent things which are in nature, the sea and the winds, and to make them serve their uses and their needs. In this way he has joined very distant people, and he has granted among different nations an image of the bond which he has placed between the parts of the same body by the veins and by the arteries.

kingdom because in this way the Germans have become the richest of all nations. But also there is profit in this, if much merchandise which is produced in the region itself is exported into other lands, for which the inhabitants then receive a large amount of money. The Germans,[2] the Spanish and the Hungarians for a long time would have been superior to the Batavians, English and French in wealth, if the merchants had not searched so greedily from foreign nations, nor would the affairs of the Spanish[3] have been likewise insignificant if the piles of gold and silver, which they dug up from America had not been wasted through ignorance and extravagance. For the English, the French and the Batavians in behalf of the merchants carried away into this kingdom do not swindle them so much of all their silver; nevertheless the Spanish were able to get every one of their own hands in their own kingdom and to invent work and uses for their relatives. However not through trade alone does wealth accede to the citizens: but also through taxes, additions of wealth are made daily to the public treasury. For I am omitting to say what a large amount of men received their nourishment for life from trade. But enough about the uses of commerce.

---

2. See, Gundlings. *Discours uber die jezigen Staaten von Europen.* T. II. cap. VI.

3. Idem T.I, cap.I sect II.

Chapter 24

For the purpose of advancing trade I shall encourage the colonies to do a lot carefully. For no land produces everything. However in the colonies, growth and merchandise produce fruits of various kinds which can be exported to foreign people who lack them. The ancient people of Tyre were not ignorant of this fact: thus it happened that they sent colonists to so many and so important remote parts of the world at that time. From this, consider Carthage, which itself was raised by numerous colonies to such a high peak of power and wealth, that, when Tyre[1] was destroyed, it remained the head of commerce. No one does not know the great fortune the Batavians produced with the wealth of trade since they sent colonists anywhere in the world. Likewise it has been established concerning the English,[2] French,[3] and Portuguese. But this is nothing concerning us. Therefore now we shall discuss a few points concerning trade because the Georgian colonists are now engaging in it and are going to in the future.

---

1. Rollins, T. XII. Concerning ancient history, p. 388.
2. Read in the Introduction to Arnold. Britische Reich.
3. Gundlings. *Europasische Staaten.* T. I, cap. II & III.

Chapter 25

However certain things must be pointed out here before we proceed to the discussion itself. First, I wish that it be noted, that I do not argue weakly concerning the value of trade which is now in Georgia, although its beginnings were insignificant, and hope lay hidden up to now as if in the grass, but once it is going to be of such a kind when more of the colony will be cultivated and it will be crowded with human beings. Second, I wish that it be considered, that I acknowledge frankly and freely that I cannot describe very accurately how much profit is going to accrue to the colonists from future commerce since the profits which are reaped from it are not going to be the same anywhere in a year. Nevertheless, when the deeds of the Georgians are compared to other colonies by the same standards by which the value of commerce is judged, I shall be able to defend my reasoning. Third, I wish it to be believed that I regard that itself to be gain which comes to the Georgians from their trade with the English, obviously they are a part of their kingdom, and it returns to their colonists. Fourth, finally I wish that it be reflected on here that Georgia extends so far and wide that the land is able to pour forth such an ample supply of products from its own territories which are not only sufficient for its inhabitants but even aid distant nations with necessities. So that the greatest importance may not seem to exceed the belief of anyone, I shall confirm it with undeniable grounds.

Chapter 26

Already it has been pointed out previously that Georgia is not less fertile than Palestine. But yet since I have convinced myself to use a lesser rather than a greater number in my reasoning so that no place may be left for doubt concerning the truth of the matter in the minds of the chosen, I shall ascribe to Georgia only a third part of the fertility where Palestine flourishes. About this therefore in the first place now it is of concern to speak. The length of Palestine[1] is said to be 400 milestones, the width in truth 25, whatever length it is drawn out, its plain extends 1,000 thousands squared. In honesty I do not even think they differ much, who affirm that land is home to 15,000,000 people. For Josephus revealed to memory that the smallest village in Galilea was crowded with 15,000 people. Since therefore truth was sought out for water at least 1,000[2] cities and towns existed in the land which is called

---

1. See Johannes Jacob Schmidt. *Biblisher Mathematicus*. P. 139-142.

2. Josephus reports that in Gallilea alone there were more than 204 cities and towns. And in the century after Christ's birth, when the Jews once again rose up against the Emperor Hadrian, there were many forts and 985 similar towns that were destroyed by the Romans. Consult I.G. Reinbecks. *Betrage Uber di Augspurg Confession* T. II, p. 127.

holy: a definite higher number is able to be found easily;[3] we submit that Galilea abounds exceedingly in the number of inhabitants before other countries. But if less confidence is held in Josephus's explanation than is adequate, we shall establish this number by setting forth arguments in another way. King Josaphat[4] who ruled scarcely a third part of all the Holy Land nevertheless led forth an army of 1,160,000 men, in this number those were not brought back who had been set in place in the cities for guards or who through helpless old age were not equal to bearing arms, whose number I estimate stood at not less than 100,000. It is clear however from the sacred writings that soldiers were chosen whose age had already reached the 20th year. From this the whole number raised was easily 3,780,000 men, who lived altogether in the Holy Land. If you were to add one wife to each of these, although however not a small number of them had more, from which there was a son[5] and daughter for each, minors up to 20 years. Besides you

---

3. John Jacob Schimdtius having been persuaded in this way believes the number of people in the Holy Land to have been 20,000,000, nevertheless he did not reckon 20 men for an entire stadium (125 paces). *Biblisch Mathematicus* p. 143. If in truth I should put back the number to 15,000,000; when all had been brought back that had to be brought back, a space at least a fourth of a Rhine land measure was left for each man of the returning ones. Compare (the book) of the most learned Johannes Gust. *Reinbeccus Betrachtung uber die Augspurgische* Concession T. III p. 124. Where he goes into the reason, how much space was made for each inhabitant of the Holy Land in a distribution into equal parts was able to be allotted if almost ten times a thousand thousand (10,000,000) were located there.

4. II, Chronic. Cap. XVII. v. 14 19.

5. B.M. Reinbeccius when from this number of men, which had lived at the time of David, he computed all the multitude of the inhabitants of the Holy Land; he counted four children, minors up to twenty years, born from each wife; although I attribute two to each in this way. See *Betrachtungen über das Augspurgische Confession* T. III p. 101.

should keep in mind, Jews not yet having reached 20 years very often were very fond of a wife and add that to the total, easily from this you can figure this number which equals to 15,000,000 besides 120,000 inhabitants (total 15,120,000). It came closely to this number which Josephus set. Because if anyone trusts all this reasoning of mine in which strangers and foreigners were not counted, he would easily understand that I have used a smaller number for a larger one.

Chapter 27

I shall now connect to Georgia the land of Canaan, which we shall discuss. Its length is 45 German miles; the width lies at 75 miles. Therefore although the plains of the Holy Land stretch 1,000 miles square, in truth Georgia's are 3,375; from this you can easily figure it exceeds Palestine three times; wherefore it has been conceded there is three times more space itself for everyone than in the (former) Palestine. Nevertheless I shall not attribute greater harvests from Georgia than those brought from the land of Canaan, aside from the fact of more forests, pastures and animals for Georgia. Since it has more space, and fills 3,375 square miles, I am omitting a harvest of tobacco, tea, coffee, sugar and spices. I predict the number of future inhabitants in Georgia not more than (5,000,000).

Chapter 28

I shall make an estimate of those things sent ahead which the Georgians were able to sell and which they themselves enjoyed. I have pointed out already in a previous place although the extent of Georgia is 3 times more than that of the Holy Land, I do not try to sell more produce from the former than products from the latter. Therefore, I shall investigate first how much wine Palestine supplied. Say, part of the Jews which I wish to estimate at 5,000,000 men did not drink even a tiny drop of wine for a whole year; nor did the remaining men (10,000,000) who did not drink excessively. I assign the families for each father, which I estimate were 1,000,000 and I lay out all in more fortunate circumstance for every single day for a drink one measure and that less than what is in our state; nor do I think that is contrary to the truth, since Judea was very productive of wine. Further on I assume 2,000,000 drained a half measure daily, and 7,000,000 every single day only drank a fourth part of the same measure; nor does my discussion now about any trade in wine which the Israelites had with their neighbors, which was by no means scorned. Therefore the production of wine in the land of Canaan was no less than 6,840,000 chomer or it filled 22,800,000 narrow amphora (jugs), each of which held 60 measures or three batos (a secondary Jewish measure).

Chapter 29

Nor do I attribute a greater supply of wine to Georgia itself. Say, the inhabitants drank 2,280,000 chomer every year or 7,600,000 amphora; there remains however 4,560,000 chomer or 15,200,000 amphora which the inhabitants can sell. Wealth, which from that comes to the English, can be seen in various ways. For the wine,[1] which is carried into England and the colonies, France and Spain receive every year from the English 50,000,000 florens. In truth it is no longer necessary for all of cultivated Georgia to export such a quantity of money from England to foreign nations: but in future time this remains in Great Britain. Because if indeed an amphora were sold by English merchants for only 25 florens, the profit of 370,000,000 florens would accede to the inhabitants themselves.[2] If anyone objects, the English are not always going to

---

1. Consult N. H. Gundlings. *European Staaten*, T.1 ch.4, para. 44, p. 642 and 35, p. 620. Where these words are: "The English buy Pontac wine in France and pay to them. Thus the Canaries and Spain lose 600,000 Ducats in business for the Canary Islands."

2. I took very careful pains to produce my arguments: but still lest I warn the reader to nausea, a too long series of numbers will tire his mind, round numbers which must be carefully noted, are less valid to consider the profits from commercial yields for the greater number, which I had found, I was able to use; thus if for the sake of example the number was presented as 100 times 1,000 times 1,000 often 100 times 1,000 which was added besides, sometimes I omitted it.

use only one kind of wine: let him consider this; since Georgia extends very widely, various kinds of wine also can be produced in it. If the English themselves do not wish to use these advantages, bear in mind, the fault can be laid on the English not on the colony.

Chapter 30

The quantity of olive oil in Georgia must be expected to be abundant. I gather from its harvest in Palestine. The way of life in Salomo[1] every day uses 300 batis of wine and 416 batis of oil. Although however this is made very clear to me, the use of oil has been more than 4 times the use of wine in Judea, nevertheless I shall maintain it is equal to wine. Think now, the inhabitants of Georgia consume as much olive oil as wine every year: thus 4,560,000 chomer or 15,200,000 amphora will be left over for sale. I estimate an amphora or 3 botos at 10 florens; from which profit returns to the Georgian colonists and the English merchants from the oil trade which equals 152,000,000 florins.

---

1. See, Johannes Jacob Schmidt. *Biblisher Mathematicus*, p. 52.

Chapter 31

I am going to compute the amount of wheat, meal, rice and other grains Georgia will produce in this way. Foreseeing God allotted a gomer of manna to each human being for food for his life, a quantity which was enough. I shall give only a half part to each inhabitant of the Holy Land every single day for his share. Thus when this calculation is begun, from which at the same time it is possible to estimate the produce for a year in the land of Canaan every single day to be 7,500,000 gomer; or 75,000 coror, or precisely every year 27,375,000 coror or 600,000,000 bushels were used up. In a similar way in Georgia I attribute a half of this size of gomer to each for food which comes out to 25,000 coror yearly in truth to 9,125,000 coror or 200,000,000 bushels. But if in truth you figure a bushel is worth 31 floren, you can put aside 600,000,000 floren in profit.

Chapter 32

Therefore the profit which at some time will be able to come forth out of Georgia, considering wine, olive oil, wheat, barley, rice, and wild oats and other grains every year will exceed 1,122,000,000 florins. Nor is this my discussion concerning trade of silk,[1] which must not be considered too lightly, flax, hemp, cotton, cochineal, indigo, cacao, as it is called, tobacco, sassafras, almond trees, quince, citrus trees; cinnamon, pepper, sugar, and other spices; further on from tea, coffee, honey, beeswax, cinere

---

1. Consult D. Riedley, "Sermon before the Lord Trustees." From Georgia we have enough flax and potash produced each year in sufficient quantity to replace 13,000 Pounds Sterling of our trade with Russia, but an even greater hope of gain is in prospect now that grape vines and mulberry trees are doing so well. This kingdom pays the Italians 300,000 Pounds for silk each year, and in Georgia one can reasonably expect more silk than we need, by which 2000 men may find work in the colony for 4 months and still more in England work the whole year through.

clavellato,[2] moss, bezoar;[3,4] next from horses, sheep and other animals; besides from fleece, skins, leather; and also from wood suitable for building ships, posts and other things, which Georgia abundantly supplies, all these can be provided to some degree. I am silent concerning gems and metals, though hope of mining in this colony is not at all impossible; also clay which a potter is said to have shaped, I do not know who; likewise marble and other precious things. I shall not bring up what comes from mining at this point, or how much increase shipping takes from this commerce or what a large number of people can be supported from it, or how many things, made in industrious England by hand, also can be brought over into Georgia. If anyone undertakes a study of all these things, he will easily recognize that the profit from all this which I have just discussed, to be greater not lower because I limited it previously. But I think I have said enough, so that it is able to be

---

2. [Editor's Note]A sort of caustic ash, used in dying and bleaching, obtained by burning distillation residue and treating the resulting ash with lime.

3. *Allerneueste Nachrichten*. p. 75 I asked the Indians whether they found no bezoar stones? I gave them a description of them and the manner in which they were found, and this is the answer: they have an abundance of them. They asked me: why do I need them. I answered: the white men use them as a medicine, and that I would buy some from them if, when I returned in a little while, it was produced. One of them produced a leather sack containing bezoar, but it was pulverized. He was a famous hunter, and assured me that this powder was very powerful for the mood and the brain; which was what it was used for most among them.

4. [Editor's Note] Gallstones of calcium and hair found in the alimentary tracts of ruminants. When immersed in arsenic laced solution, a bezoar will remove the toxic compounds. Used until the 18th century as a preventative against being poisoned.

understood that Georgia is second[5] to no colony also in the consideration of commerce.

---

5. Thus I assign all the profit which comes from Georgia to equal 2,000,000,000 florens, of that I shall leave half part of the profits to the inhabitants of Georgia, the rest to the English. By this reasoning, if I shall distribute the profit equally among every single Georgian, every year 20 florins. In truth the Indies make somewhat more profit, 32 cruciferis, you should wonder less about that, because the boys and also the girls produce such outstanding work in various kinds of labors, especially in preparing silk (which indeed is confirmed from *The Newest Commentary of the Georgian Affair* p. 73) that they take no more pay than for their living and food. Indeed not so much from their own work goes to the slaves (uncultured workers); truly what they lack comes to their masters, so that on both sides to such a degree an equal division is made. From this computation I do not think I have falsified the results. For by this agreement an amount can be found with no great difficulty, how much profit yearly for a different number of inhabitants can be hoped for from Georgia. For if it is determined concerning the number of inhabitants; when computation has been made, it is discovered that the profit reaches 5,000 florens. However when the entire profit has been found, which every inhabitant of Georgia reaps, and that part of the profit comes forth which falls to the advantage of Great Britain and the English colonies, obviously that comes in equal parts of profit with the inhabitants of Georgia. It can be easily collected in an adequate manner how much oil, wine, grain, and other things of this kind, for a different kind of inhabitants can be exported anywhere in a year to foreigners. For innumerable colonies harvest so much produce from their own farms that with what is sold, it yields not only the necessities for themselves but also for 2,000 foreigners. I shall point this out clearly by an example: consider, 50,000 inhabitants are in Georgia, thus they take a profit of 10,000,000 florens from the revenue, equal to this is the profit of England and the other English colonies. Those 50,000 Georgian colonists are able to delight 100,000 foreigners with wine, oil, grain, and other fruits, so that the inhabitants hold back one third part, they take two thirds for foreigners. However, I think after twenty years this number must be computed again, common sense itself will establish it, with the

number of inhabitants having been increased, the Georgia venture will be extremely profitable. Because however if anyone claims the fertility of Georgia is the same as that of Canaan, he is easily being too generous, because the 50,000 inhabitants of Georgia on that which I grant to be a third less fertile than the land of Canaan are able to provide a grain supply for 400,000 foreigners. Georgia however is able to produce such a fertile supply of fruit and grain that it can export so much to others without any detriment to its citizens. What is gathered from it, because the land, uncultivated before, in the space of a few years will produce with most ample fertility and it will bring in ready harvests: since indeed the nature of Canaan, as it now is, has become so harsh and horrible, some writers debate its first fertility, not with vehemence. Compare the author of Britifchen Reichs p. 646. If the inhabitants of Carolina (This applies also to Georgia, which was a part of Carolina, however, it surpasses it in fruitfulness and opportunities for commerce in several areas) were hard-working, so wealth will flow to him. For I have been assured that one with 500 Pounds Sterling, invested smartly in Carolina as the same amount in England, would in a few years live in as much plenty as a person in England with 300 Pounds Sterling a year. And if he invests this flow with suitable care, then he will, without needing any stinginess, come to great wealth.

Chapter 33

We proceed from the first three reasons, for which the colonies had been established, encouraged, and let loose, in order now to the fourth and last for which they have been set up. In truth we place this of the remaining reasons in defense of the regions of some kingdom suitable to it. This reason especially compelled the Romans to send men into colonies. For Livy[1] reports this: "Treachery to the city and a future land for the seas sent out the battle standards, circuses and colonists." Tacitus also has this about colonies: "A colony is established in conquered lands, a place of strength against rebels and tainted associates for the official service of the laws." What? Because I am able to cite our country itself as a witness of this matter. Let its name alone show this because it was assumed from Augustus[2] the General, who having conquered the Rhaetii and the Vindelicii, and having captured our city itself, immediately sent colonists into it by this plan, so that these tribes could throw off the yoke of savagery from their necks with more difficulty. Nor are examples lacking of very recent times. Thus

---

1. Libro I, cap.LVI.
2. See, that most generous man, Pauli A. Stetten. *Geschichte der H. Romerischen Reichs freyen Stadt Augspurg*, c. II, p. 6 & following.

Cuba[3] has been a fortress of the Spanish, in America and Batavia[4] of the Batavians in Asia: for if war is started in these regions with these tribes, this bastion ought to be overcome before the others.

---

3. Gundlings. *Discours uber die jezigen Staaten von Europen.* T. I, p. 132, et seq.
4. Idem T. I, p.813.

Chapter 34

It only remains that I show briefly that our colony is a fortification for the English. That is immediately apparent from the location[1] of the colony itself. The next door neighbor, Florida, limits the English colonies on the continent; so that neither the French nor the Spanish, unless they should occupy it first, would be able to make an attack on the others. From its very nature it seems an

---

1. *Britisches Reich* V. 1 p. 673 and 674. The happy outlook that this colony had in its foundation, and which we have laid out at length, will seem to an English reader amazing, especially if he has a clear understanding of the great part that such a settlement brings to the security of our other American colonies from stable land and to the business of the nation. Its situation shows what a protection it is against the Spanish, and its capital, Savannah, lies no more than 150 miles from St. Augustine, the capitol of Spanish Florida, and a great interference to English business between this province and the Gulf of Mexico. This serves to strengthen the border, since it is the border of all its colonies in North America, and thus its care and protection is of the entire essence, and not just a calming help, to the business and might and honor of the kingdom more than any other. Thus all are safer when this place is safer. And if a dock or port is made at the border of the province, and it is done with suitable security, so ought no more harm come to our American colonies and business. And at this time, so strikingly supplied with the needs of ship building, many places have built ships themselves, and there is no doubt that such work, with people and businesses, is ever increasing. What an assist to the Mississippi trade this is evident.

excellent fortification. For whether an attack is made on land or by sea: the forest surrounds it on the side of the land as though it were closed, and besides the Indians themselves bound by the closest chains of friendship to the English keep them away; this very great difficulty of approaching stops them. They tested both in the year 1742. The Spanish were driven back most easily: more will be said about this fact at a later time. For actually unless Georgia should be placed at that time as a fortification against the Spanish, in the opinion of everyone, Carolina would be in the power of the Spanish. For this very same reason they decided to name Georgia the American Gibraltar; and a delegate of the dead king of the Spaniards openly acknowledged: his own king (Madrito), by his own right preferred to yield that to Georgia, because it was a wise and excellent idea, even if it was done by the enemy, by which it is evidence enough that in Georgia are situated the fortunes[2] of all the other colonies in America which belong to the English.

---

2. Lord Bishop Riedley preached: What we care to do for the security and prosperity of other colonies, that is also a reason to care for this (namely Georgia) The ease with which ships can be sailed and its quiet bays and harbors, where they can enter and stay safely, with the special advantage that they are free of the American worm, which is the death of West-Indian ships, shows well enough what benefits Great Britain will have from forthright help to the colony. Let us not through indifference or inaction toward helping this bastion of British rule, lose the advantage, which we would otherwise have, and which could be much greater in the future. It lies so that it is the key to closing or opening the path of the fleet of New Spain and the Galleon from Panama depending on the conditions of the times and the behavior of our sometimes enemy.

Chapter 35

Although four reasons have been considered why colonies have been established at all times, the constitution and administration of each colony must differ in a few ways. The superiority of Georgia over others is apparent even here in many ways. Certainly it was not unimportant or inconsequential that the greater part of all the other colonies were conquered by strength of arms and indeed were polluted either by the blood of the old inhabitants or of the new colonists; Georgia is free of this blame and disgrace. Whom did the immense cruelty of the Spanish in subjugating America and the slaughter of innumerable clearly innocent human beings put to flight? How many wars flared up among the Spanish, Lusitanian, English, and Batavians[1] in Asia until the Batavians had established and made secure their colonies in that part of the world? How many skirmishes occurred with the British and the Indians[2] in New England, Virginia and Carolina? What fights and struggles arose about the Philippine Islands and Indonesia; so that you discover almost no colony which was not the cause of murder, where the old inhabitants were destroyed by massacre in a pitiful manner. In truth our Georgia was established not only without any letting of blood, but the English even declared peace in the beginning by a treaty with the Indians who not a little before struck Carolina to the north.

---

1. See Gundlings, *Discours uber die jezigen Staaten von Europen.* T. I, cap. V, para. 32 & 33 p.111 et seq.
2. See. *Das Britische Reich in America*, and those capitals of the same, where it is discussed about England, Virginia and Carolina.

Chapter 36

Since in truth I am shut out by a lack of time so that I cannot publish more about this preeminence of Georgia over other colonies, I am moving my foot forward to the productive importance in which the superiority of the Georgia colony shines out. However it examines this in this way, that all children[1] of the colonists, even those born from strangers in Georgia and however many are born from them, equally in England itself and in the other colonies they enjoy all the same rights, privileges and laws, in which the English themselves delight; and the king of England has commanded all the colonists of Georgia to be free from and responsible to no other laws except those which were brought by the rulers of that colony, however these themselves must agree closely to English law. It is well known indeed that the Romans presented some colonies with citizenship: however at this time I do not know of any colony which rejoices in this immunity. Now I could be long winded in adding up profits which will come to the inhabitants from this law of the state, except the narrowness of space left to me for the rest orders me to pull in my sails.

---

1. *Neueste Nachricht von Georgien*, p. 60.

Chapter 37

Therefore let us hasten to the third superiority of Georgia, which is placed here, because the administration of this one colony was handed over to a board as a whole of very wise and splendid men. That is something certainly no colony is able to assume for itself. If you mention to me the colonies of Batavians in Asia, for whose administration a special board was established; you will remember, any decision of this board was far away. That has been established for the ruling of all[1] the colonies of Asia, of which there is not an exact number: the official duty of this is that it secures the safety of Georgia. The former was first undertaken to promote trade alone; the latter especially to produce care of those poor people, who because of a purer practice of their religion were pushed out of their native land. In that no one followed, unless he turned over a certain sum of money for common use to the East Indian Mercantile Society, and let it seize the fruit of the profit from this enterprise: on the other hand, the Georgians having been put in charge of all the profit of the colony, which came from it, they themselves wanted to be in charge. Because however if any one derives for himself of his own free will enormous problems without any hope of profit; truly he must be considered to be led only by love of the republic for the purpose of providing the safety of many men: since usually those who hope for profit from their

---

1. See Gundlings, *Discours uber die jezigen Staaten von Europen.* T. I, cap. V, para. 38, p. 838.

province, only look for an appropriate opportunity. In truth how much more wholesome are those decisions which proceed from love toward others, than those which the private opportunity of each man suggests. For this reason the growth of this colony in so short and so dangerous a time is exceptional enough because it offers outstanding testimony about the constant concern, untiring zeal, and excellent plans of the trustees.

Chapter 38

In truth this name[1] has been given by the English to that society itself to which had been entrusted the concern of ruling Georgia. The Common Council of the Trustees of the colony of Georgia in America, which is thus rendered in Latin: commune consilium curatorum, caloniae Georgianae in America. This is established by the Magistrates and the princes of the Kingdom England, priests, knights and others, all of singular wisdom and prudence who are brought forward by praise[2] into one group. Nine of them were chosen as trustees, no matter how many weeks they assemble for the smallest reason, and they bring together their plans concerning the development and safety of Georgia. Every year individual members of this society deliberate in general in London about the daily affairs and the situation in Georgia, and appoint new comrades to their own order. Power has also been given to this group to seek and collect donations from the wealth of the English citizens for the public use of the colony of Georgia; although both governing bodies of the kingdom have made a gift of their own free will already many thousands of gold coins for this purpose.

---

1. Or even: Trustees For Establishing the Colony of Georgia in America.
2. See *Neueste Nachricht von Georgien*. p. 15. This honorable society or corporation was established by His Majesty of Great Britain in June 1732, with a privilege, in English called a charter, confirmed by Parliament granting to this true governor and his followers the full control of this spacious province of Georgia.

Chapter 39

Also by the help of God, and everything being cared for cautiously by this very wise group of trustees, the fact is, that in fifteen years, even among the blare of the trumpets and the racket of armed men, this colony has received so much growth that now recently many cities are seen being built, of which the most important is Savannah.[1] Augusta comes next, Augusta Ebenezer,[2] the

---

1. Neuest Nachricht von Georgien. p. 20 & 21. the capitol on the banks of the Savannah River is laid out to be very regular and spacious. In the extension of this town, it is fine as far as one goes, that one already sees quite a few broad streets which houses laid out according to the plan, all well built according in form, symmetry and uniformity and fitting the nature of the land. The number of these houses seems to be almost a few hundred, which new structures appearing to increase daily. Similarly, a church, the quai for landing cargo and a textile factory will soon be finished. There is also a chancery or office set up that had 3 office workers. It is amazing how populous this town is in consideration of the short time it has been laid out. It lies about 10 English miles from the sea on high ground and for about 5 or 6 English miles the land behind it and certainly for a mile along the river is strong and fruitful, altogether a very suitable area and a well chosen site. The water from the river, over 100 feet wide in front of the town, is fresh, and springs rise from the side of the hills. Ships drawing 12 feet of water can lie at anchor within 40 feet of the bank. Opposite the town is an island of very rich pastures, where a large herd of livestock can be kept.

2. *Britisches Reich in America* T. I p.671. It lies in a strong and fruitful land, where an acre of ground produces almost 30 bushels of

city of Joseph,[3] Darien,[4] Frederica,[5] The fort of S. Andrea, Purisburg,[6] Oldfort. The Scotch fort, Palachocolas, with no villages as Abercorn and the others.

Indian corn. And in the last year, 100,000 loads of skins were brought here.
    3. It came from Scottish colony. *Neueste Nachricht von Georgien.*
    4. In any case, by Scotlanders laid down. l.c. p. 24.
    5. Fort Frederica on the island of St. Simon is a regular fortress, with four bastions and a trench, and with some outworks, which is surrounded with a cedar pallisade, and the ramparts are covered with sod. A town is set behind the fort and is itself laid out in an orderly way. There are now several villages on the island of St. Simon and the town of Frederica is very much improved. L.c. p. 24 & 25.
    6. *Ebenezer Nachrichten.* T. I, p. 143.

Chapter 40

Since indeed no republic endures in good repair without laws, they say: and this one itself was about to threaten error and ruin, if its safety had not been strengthened with laws; which, as I perceive, time and space do not allow to make known. I refer the reader to *Commentaries on Salzburger Affairs*, and *The Newest Description of Georgia*, in which it is described accurately in detail both what laws the colonists used, and how much land each one received. I am unable to pass over in silence, however, this one law, where it is safe, no slaves are introduced in this colony, this sentiment had to be repeated from the constitution itself of the colony. Clearly it was established so that poor people would be able to make a living for themselves there, a thing which, truly, slaves, because of a cheap price, where their labor is allowed, very often take from them. Very wisely therefore this was the plan of the trustees of the colony, as you repeat also in prayers by men, who think about this more carefully, what would be more useful for them, and for the world, aroused in the same way, they made a demand of introducing slaves[1] into this colony for no one, and they ratified everlasting power and authority for this law.

---

1. I speak of the great unrest among slaves. Carolina proves an example for us. *Ebenezerische. Nachricht.* T. 2 p. 44. Now the people of Carolina are disquieted and in much need, around 60 Negroes fled together, killed some people dead, and ran into the forest and perhaps all the way to the Spanish. His excellency, Lord General Oglethorpe, sent guns, powder and lead here, that is to Ebenezer, because a number of the

moorish slaves in Carolina had seized weapons, set may houses on fire, plundered and slaughtered the people, and he is worried that they will cross the Savannah river and come into the colony.

Chapter 41

But should anyone perhaps say, lest it be spoiled, indeed that the Georgia colony was able to be so perfected by the greatest care, which is now under consideration, so that it is second to none: we must be concerned lest the more negligent English ever evaded their responsibilities. Indeed whoever argues this way, I wish he would consider how much profit returns to England from the colonies; with how much concern how much work sometimes they established the colonies; and once established they kept them safe, increased them, and brought them to completion; as far as the persistence of the Indians who made attacks against the colonies, and pushed forward violence and revenge, the English were not stopped by these attacks, as a matter of fact, although the old colonists were destroyed by massacre by the Indians, they always sent new people into the colonies, who by persistence of their spirits recaptured the colonists taken by the weapons of the enemy, and preserved others already snatched from the enemy, in these matters they were an example in readiness; as it is established concerning the Island which has the name Providence,[1] the French were forced by arms to restore it. Just as it is recognized in the present war that the promontory of Breton having been seized by force of arms from the French was a concern dear to them. Wherefore although it did not escape the notice of the English to take as much profit from

---

1. See Gundlings, *Discours uber die jezigen Staaten von Europen.* T. I, p. 627.

the Georgian trade as they could: it would have been necessary to first change their character than that they should walk away from all concern of Georgia. What? Because the English although first of all they were going to have no greater amount of English trade for that reason however do not fear neglect of this colony, since especially it acted for the defense of other colonies from the attacks of the enemy, because indeed irreparable harm would come for the English from it, if this colony were to come into the power of the enemy. I submit that before it was necessary to dissolve and desert that most splendid society which was established and confirmed in this plan by the king, that it would promote Georgia anywhere in a suitable way, rather than that there be any fear concerning the death of Georgia. Because before that happened anticipating the status of England to be changed, although inwardly it ought to be turned around. It happens that divine providence has guarded the safety of Georgia thus far and also will guard it without interruption since this colony was established for the glory of God and also for accomplishing both temporal and eternal safety of many human beings. All of which produces undoubted hope of growth.

Chapter 42

Those things, which I have previously said, put before the eyes of the kind reader the way of the government in Georgia. Now indeed I shall comment, however very briefly on affairs carried out in that colony. First the Knight and Governor Jacob Oglethorpe, who was sent into Georgia in the month of February 1733, lay the foundation of his colony and began to establish his metropolis to which he gave the name Savannah. Others followed this city of which I have already mentioned earlier. In truth the trustees wanted this colony to provide safety from a hostile attack in a double way. At first they entered into treaties with the Indians as a group who lived in Georgia: then they built more forts throughout the whole colony. This plan did not disappoint them. For the Indians, most hostile before to the English living in Carolina, now gave many evidences of firm friendship to this colony. Indeed the forts were a great protection to the colonists when the Spanish threatened a hostile attack against this colony so that the Spanish were denied all hope of bringing Georgia back into its own wealth. Then fortune deprived them of their huge hopes: truly it happened this way, that that divine providence which shines forth greatly, fortified the heart of the very brave Governor Oglethorpe with such courage and wisdom that with short supplies he not only attacked a tenfold[1] greater

---

1. What pertains to the hostile attack of the Spanish against Georgia: we believe certain things from the letters written by the Knight Oglethorpe to be omitted not to be from this affair. *Ebenezerishce Nachricht.* v. 2 p.

number of the enemy but even defeated them. Wherefore it is a fact that now indeed the Spanish would not dare approach this colony.

1261. God has through the revelation of his word delivered us from the hands of the Spanish who came with 14 sails of small galleys and other boats made attacks in the Cumberland Sound; but flight and fear from the Lord overcame them and they fled. The Spanish also came with another mighty fleet of 36 ships and vessels in the Jekyll sound, and were, after a sharp battle, master of it, since we had only our people: confidently in such an unequal fight, since we had only 4 vessels to set against their might. However, God was a shield for our people; without which in such an unequal battle, we held out at one time for 4 hours, not one of ours was killed, although many of the others were lost, and five were killed by a single shot. They landed with 4,500 troops on the island according to the report of prisoners and even those English who escaped from them. The first party marched through the forest near the city, Frederica, as God delivered them into the hands of a small number of ours, they fought and were destroyed and fled. Another party, supporting them, fought as well, but were soon destroyed. We might with truth say that the hand of God fought with us, since in the two conflicts more than 500 were killed for 50, but still the enemy fought bravely for a long time, especially their Grenadiers fought with great bravery, however, their ships did little damage, so much so that at the same time not one of us was killed, but the enemy was brought to disorder, and with great spirit pursued. Also, according to the account of those taken prisoner over 200 Spanish never returned to their camp. They also came with their other galleys against the city, and pulled back again, without a single shot fired. Later a fright overcame them, and they fled and left behind some cannon and many other things that they had captured. 28 sail attacked fort William, where there were only 50 men, and after a three hour attack, they gave up and left the province, and they were chased up the St. John's. Altogether in the entire expedition and great armed attack of the Spanish no more than [number unclear] of ours were captured or killed. We may with truth say that the Lord has done a great thing for us, that he has saved us from the hands of a countless enemy, that we, already convinced in his thoughts and at peace, that would have tormented and burned us. & p. 1263 to 1264. The aforesaid officers, who spoke with me, told me that the Spanish soldiers carried letters of indulgence from the Pope for their sins of 7 years, if they overcame, killed and burned heretics. They had a large quantity of hand, foot and neck irons with them, in which to put their captives; because the attack was in their opinion certain of success, and they would seize the inhabitants of this colony.

Chapter 43

Indeed this affair, about which I have already spoken, affected the whole colony. But when each and every citizen has been declared expert: I fear I would be more obliging in injustice, if I should describe them by counting up. Because of this I shall stick to one town whose fate I am going to set forth very briefly. It is Ebenezer of the Salzburgers. I have already indicated before that this city was situated in a most charming[1] region. But time afterwards taught them it was too humid for the same kind of agriculture,[2] it was especially suited for grazing cattle. For this reason the Salzburgers, although they had built many huts and four homes there, having gathered supplies and having left their old dwellings, in which they had lived for the space of two years, established a new city, which they called *New Ebenezer* so that they distinguished it from the old. While they were laying the foundations for the new city, sufficient and very fertile land was distributed to them, afterwards into cultivating this the Salzburgers threw all their work and concern. From which it is a fact that they not only took nourishment from their farms, but some was even left over which they sold to others.

---

1. *Ebenezerische. Nachricht.* T.1, p.80. I traveled to the area of Ebenezer, a place 21 miles from Savannah city and 30 miles from the sea, where one finds a river, small hills, a clear stream and cold springs and much grass.

2. *Ebenezerische Nachricht* T. 1. p.2003 & 2004.

Chapter 44

It is more remarkable that among the cultivated land they did not also stop erecting public buildings. First among them was an orphanage in which widows, orphans and other poor people of the Salzburgers were received. Then this building for a long space of time was used as a church. Immediately from the beginning more than 20 human beings were cared for in it: as the number increased every year, it was necessary that they construct more buildings. Then they built churches, one in the town, another in the country, at the first they gave the name Jerusalem, to the other Mt. Zion. Next they built mills for diverse uses, two indeed for milling grain, and for grinding rice; one of these was used when the supply of water was more plentiful, the other, when it was lacking. Besides these two, they also built a third in which trees were cut into boards and planks, some for building, others for selling. Nor shall I talk about bridges built, public roads constructed, about earthworks laid down on the shore of the rapid river against the march of the tides, or other buildings erected for public use. It happened that every single father of a family built his own home[1] suitable for himself both in the city and in the country.

---

1. Anyone who wants more accurate information about all this, should read *Ebenezerifchen Nachrichten*.

Chapter 45

Since all this was established in a space of twelve years, the material for everything was prepared and brought up by the inhabitants themselves, if anyone considers rightly in his mind, he cannot help but admire greatly the increase of the fortunes of the Salzburgers in America and acknowledge their daily most outstanding labor. However that future would have been much greater if a delay had not been thrown in sometimes. The first location of the city was on marshy land where the arable land did not respond to the wishes of the colonists. For within two years after they began to build a new city, the newly cultivated land having been deserted, all the space of former time, and all the previous labor was in vain and it fell down uselessly wasted. Also for the first years almost all the Salzburgers for a long time were slow about their occupations being held down by fevers. Especially when they began to build the new city, much time slipped by until farms were divided for them. Then also hope of planting crops, created by unpredictable weather often frustrated the inexperienced. Afterwards there was no one who could clearly show them how silk ought to be prepared and how grapevines ought to be handled and cultivated: at last by holding onto all teachable skills they conquered, and will conquer in the future. It was this very understanding and for this reason the Salzburgers had some things abundantly before the rest of the Georgians. Especially however this was accepted and also attributed to a Divine gift and to the generosity of many benefactors, because from many kingdoms, chiefly in truth from Germany as a rule innumerable benefits were brought in to the Salzburgers. For from the time when they settled in Georgia, many thousands of florens were sent across the sea to them as aid. For the incredible ardor of the backers and the enthusiasm in many benefactors for giving again and again in no way was extinguished so that rather when an occasion was presented it was inflamed more and more. Now large gifts were brought by hand for the purpose of building the orphanage and for caring for human beings in it; now for building another church in the town; now in truth for other buildings some public, some private. Indeed the Salzburgers cherished this generosity and incredible enthusiasm in hope with eternal, memorable and grateful devotion as much as in God and in the trustees, and they freely said the size of these kindnesses were so large in hope that no gratitude of spirit was equal in expression of approval: although they would pray indeed both publicly and privately to God for their Trustees, for whom they would request daily fortunate happenings. Besides in truth among those unusual evidences of divine providence, for the lasting safety and security of Salzburger affairs evidence of care and vigilance was held to be outstanding and that itself because for many years now both on land and sea the English and Spanish were in a raging war. Although many English ships were captured by the enemy indeed not one of these was intercepted which brought chests loaded with gifts into Georgia for the Saltzbugers, since indeed one or more ships loaded with gifts coming to aid the needs and wants of the Salzburgers were sent almost anywhere that year. And since the affairs of the Salzburgers were not yet so refined that they did not need the aid and help of others, and moreover we were encouraged to a hope of trading whence they could provide a living and clothing and other necessary things for themselves. As yet that would be in the future, for recently fortune dealt them a serious blow, because a certain sly old man, having raised the greatest hope of very lucrative trade, about carrying to Jamaica and Barbados' grain having already been made into flour, secretly stole from them, whence the affair did no little damage to the Salzburgers, all our hope has been placed in God, who wished to impose this mind to the Trustees, that again they lighten this calamity of the Salzburgers by their generosity, I am certainly persuaded that they, who brought kindness to others, will be rewarded in the same manner by God, or in a greater way; because we hold that as much as possible in our desired prayers.

Chapter 46

And these are generally the things which pertained to the civil affairs of the Salzburgers in Georgia, but it is also necessary to say something about their church. Change brought into the colony of Georgia considerable enthusiasm for spreading among the Indians a purer understanding of God. Immediately in the beginning when the English began to establish this colony, a certain chief of these Indians, by name Tomo Cachi, having gone to England with the noble Oglethorpe, asked that he himself be instructed with his people in the sciences, arts, and religion of the English, indeed with the knowledge of the divine God. However up to now the outcome has not entirely answered our prayers, since this situation has been complicated by the many difficulties. First among these, is that the words themselves cannot be understood without very great difficulty.[1] Meanwhile however new policies[2] of the Georgia governor are arriving about filling their souls with Christian doctrine. Indeed also the outcome everywhere was not equal to the policies, and more favorable hope and somewhat less tenuous success is offered, especially although the name of Christians was

---

1. *Ebenezerische Nachricht.* T. I . 382.
2. See *Ebenezerische Nachricht.* T.2 p. 1142. The Lord Trustees are concerned that the heathens, who are friendly to the English, be given the opportunity to know Christ, the Savior of the World, and accordingly they have asked Colonel Stephens and Master Jones to bring their good work through another effort to a completion.

previously hateful to the Indians, many of the colonists, among these especially the Salzburgers, shed light on them by the observation of their customs, their goodness rendered many acceptable. In New England conversion of the Indians to the Christian religion was not at all infrequent, although in the beginning of the establishment of the colony that hope was very small. Nor were they forced by violence but of their own accord as suppliants they came to ask that they be instructed in the precepts of the Christian religion. In a similar manner also in Georgia the spotty seed of the Christian religion has not yet blossomed into a crop: in divine work I have certain hope of a most fruitful outcome.

Chapter 47

Because the status of the church directs attention to the rest of Georgia: indeed in considering this, Georgia certainly yields to no other colony. For of these *The Governors and the Society for Telling forth the Knowledge of Christ*, whose labors in this matter cannot be praised enough, took all concern that when divine words were given to the pastors, when they had been carefully instructed in heavenly doctrine, then the holiness of every single life was noticed, each was considered for the safety of souls: that is how it was done, and thus far is done everyday. Frequent letters of the Salzburgers sent to Europe testify to this very fact, in which, as they can, they give the greatest thanks to God, because the interpreters of the divine words and the holy men of wisdom, with whom the safety of their souls was in the first place, contributed greatly. Then in truth even civil affairs were a concern to their hearts. This concern brought it about that the Salzburgers give examples of outstanding piety, and some others can see the beginning of Christianity in their customs, as if in a mirror. Ecclesiastical discipline thrived as greatly as possible in this beginning; since they publicly disapproved of those who cursed, spendthrifts and gluttons and as many as soaked themselves in wine, or wherever those in any way committed an open scandal, or showed hatred by burning their own possessions as a matter of fact in no way even as matters now stand are they buried in sacred ground, nor before they turn over a new leaf, is use of this sacred grass again given to them. Still their pastors never stop preaching to them daily about divine matters either publicly or in private. Whence it happens that the Salzburgers say that they are much more fortunate in this wilderness than if they had flocked to a country with all enticements, they follow their leaders with unusual affection; even after the death of one, named Israel Christian Gronau, who in the year 1745 departed this life for eternal light, to make it so evident, that when the announcement of his death was received, no one spoke who did not pour forth tears in complaint. In his place Herman Henrick Lemkenius followed who was not second in honesty, virtue and religion to the deceased, to John Martin Bolzio, unusually endowed with knowledge of sacred literature and wisdom, was given the congregation. Then he delayed coming to this place from Germany; he was very often held back by weakness of his body. Then in truth overwhelmed by the weight of the negotiations (obviously he was performing the priestly duties of sacred things and the work of a magistrate[1] excellently) his good health was spoiled; from which he was permitted to understand the singular providence of God which took charge of his life. If you discount the highest trustees of the colony, almost to this man alone is owed recognition that from 600 difficulties and problems, with which he wrestled, relying on divine help, he surmounted especially arduous circumstances, from which scarcely no other person, unless he had known despair, would have undertaken and brought to completion for the safety and comfort of the Salzburgers. Therefore truly it happened to him as it is said of Joseph in sacred literature: "Everything that he began, ended well and favorably."

---

1. See, *Ebenezerische Nachricht*. T.II. p. 1991. From Lord General Oglethorpe I received a really very friendly letter before three days, in which he sought to persuade me with many arguments, not, as was in Witlens, to take upon myself outside duties and nightly offices, but to undertake this burden gladly.

Chapter 48

Attention ought not to pass over in silence what the illustrious knight and Trustee Jacob Ogelthorpe did for the safety of the Germans in the city of Frederica. For likewise this man who also had the safety of Georgia especially in his heart, avoided no labor for its comfort, and avoided danger in wars waged in Georgia with the Spanish, a most happy outcome, at his own expense he provided a pastor whose name was Drieslero, for holding and encouraging the Germans at Frederica who were dedicated to the Lutheran religion. Afterwards in going over this sacred responsibility of his duties, he allowed nothing of faithfulness to be omitted. At the end of the past year snatched from human affairs, he departed to God.

Chapter 49

Besides these things also that orphanage, most worthy of memory was established in Georgia by a certain herald of the divine word called Whitefield. For he, after looking carefully at the children in Georgia wither who were bereft of parents or destitute of wealth, established an orphanage[1] by soliciting a large number of gifts. Here he accepted children of this kind to which he added some Indians. Nor did this orphanage receive too little growth at that time; by the kind help of God, his reputation and the well being of the poor were changed in it, indeed in later times the orphanage will receive more honors and children.

---

1. See, *Ebenezerische Nachricht*. T.II. p. 1991. It calls itself the Waysenhaus Inn and is known as a princely place, and the inhabitants enjoy many comforts. And God's word and prayers are industriously practiced there.

Chapter 50

But enough already, as much as is able to be accomplished through the weakness of my talent has been said by me about the excellence of Georgia. Nothing is left over, other than that for the constant increase of this colony, of all the colonists, especially of the Salzburgers, for everlasting safety, for sending our pastors among the Indians, finish however, for the greatest good luck of the most generous and most outstanding governor for this colony, and of all the trustees, by extending recognition of the word of Christ, let us now publicly express our solemn vows. May the divine prediction which appears in Deuteronomy Chapter 28 verses 3, 4, 5, 10, 11, 12, and 13 come to pass for these one at a time and as a group. "You will be blessed in the city, blessed in the country, blessed will be the fruit of your womb, of the ground, of your cattle, first of the herds then the young of your bleating flocks. Blessed will be your wicker baskets and your kneading troughs; blessed will you be when you come in; blessed when you go out. And so God will scatter before you your enemies who will rise up against you so that having approached you on one road, they will flee before you on seven roads. The Lord will open to you the treasury of his goods, the sky; he will send down rain on your land in its season, and he will prosper all your works, and you will lend to many peoples, but you yourselves will not borrow; and he will make you the head not the tail, and you will be more advanced not less advanced, if only you will obey the commandments of your God Jehovah which I command to you today, that you take care to do them."

Epilogue

The guardian of unusual ability and of great expectation to the young man
—Johannes Augustus Urlsperger

Four years have passed, most charming Urlsperger, in which you have been committed to my trust and adroitness. Your very esteemed parent committed you who held you; his embrace was with most tender love, he accomplished this most difficult task so that your genius would be taught correctly and by seizing the accomplishments of this most outstanding ability it would be developed diligently and in a mature way. He was not unaware that all hope of future years must be taken from the first formation of life. And now he entrusted your mind to my care in order that it would be more polished in those studies which are necessary for it which would hasten to hand over genuine instruction quickly and correctly. Divine grace provided you with outstanding endowments of mind. Therefore since you had been handed over to my instruction extraordinary passion for learning has been discovered in you, for proceeding with humanitarian letters and other studies which scholars ought to have. And indeed so great was that enthusiasm of yours that while through that entire space of time in which you devoured the rules of wisdom from my mouth, you proved your earnestness to me by exercises of various kinds and by tireless passion for learning to which you added the charm of your habits. You received the unusual support of the most kind rulers of our school whom God having endowed with all kinds of good things has supported them thus far generously for a very long time. Now your diligence shows itself publicly at last. You are able to clearly point out by an equal and devoted proof to the reader how much you have accomplished in these studies. But since we are carefully educated every day by experience, how many mistakes and crises the age of youth may have, which makes the way of adolescence precarious, and slipping down hill. Moreover, those who dedicate themselves to literature today, since there are not enough intelligent practices of this generation, they are deceived by the ridicule of the most useless opinions, and they follow phantoms and worthless ideas of things; in truth they are neglected. You by the aid of divine grace having glided by these rocks followed those things which are most truthful and especially good and genuine in education. At some time or other they will do a lot of good to you and to others because you have worked hard to imbue your mind with knowledge. I congratulate most highly with all my heart your wise parent concerning such outstanding hope for his son: whom I certainly believe is going to be a sweet comfort of his old age and whom young and vigorous he yielded by the mercy of heaven for the good of the universal church. Now you will go away into nurturing Eberhardin, just as if you were going to migrate into a new colony, and there you will render assistance to more holy knowledge by your enthusiasm. He is not able to teach others who himself has not published something first; wherefore, whether truth has to be strengthened or whether falsehood has to be refuted and restrained, it is necessary that you first fill up your mind with learning, without the protection of that neither is able to be set right. Now I say repeatedly that by innocence of life and especially by practice of morals you strengthen yourself by example before you teach. Since these two cannot be separated, you will be careful that destined for sacred service, you will take equal care of life and learning, and once brought to the same conclusion you will furnish a clear example of teaching and living just as if those committed to your care looking into a mirror are turned away from wickedness by your words and deeds. I order that this may turn out happily, and in order that, as I predict, you may bring forth a great many sacred and literary works and they may be suitable and special: we can ask for as much grace as possible from God by our prayers and vows, I pray for you from my heart for most fruitful and abundant blessing.

Farewell

Written in school on the seventh day of September 1747.

About the Translator

Theodora Heinsohn (Warner) Miller had a long interest in Latin. She taught Latin in junior high and high school in Cullman, Ala., and St. Simon's Island, Ga., earning her master's degree at the University of Georgia at the same time her two youngest children were earning theirs. Part of her coursework involved study in Greece and Italy. For her master's thesis, she translated all the works of Hrotsvit of Gandersheim, a 10th century Saxon canoness and playwright who wrote in Latin.

She took on the translation of Johannes Urlsberger's book about the Georgia colony at the request of the Salzburger Society of Savannah. The book, written in Latin in 1747, had been in the Emory University library for years but no one had translated it.

A native of Charleston, S.C. (born 1923), a longtime resident of coastal Georgia and a lifelong Lutheran, Mrs. Miller had an interest in the Salzburgers, German Lutherans who sought religious freedom in Oglethorpe's colony. During the years she spent translating the book, she made several visits to the former settlement 20 miles west of Savannah, site of the nation's first orphanage and old folk's home. On one of those trips, she met several Indian families who recounted stories of their ancestors' interaction with the Salzburgers in colonial times that had been passed down through the generations.

Mrs. Miller lived in Burlington, N.C. until her death in June 2007. She is survived by five children and eleven grandchildren.

www.ingramcontent.com/pod-product-compliance
Lightning Source LLC
Chambersburg PA
CBHW030116010526
44116CB00005B/267